# STYLE IN ART

*. . . a philosophy of art is steri-
lized unless it makes us aware of
the function of art in relation
to other modes of experience.*

**JOHN DEWEY**

# STYLE IN ART
## THE DYNAMICS OF ART AS CULTURAL EXPRESSION

## by LINCOLN ROTHSCHILD

New York  •  Thomas Yoseloff, *Publisher*  •  London

Library of Congress Catalog Card Number: 60–13622


Thomas Yoseloff, Inc.
11 East 36th Street
New York, 16, N.Y.


Thomas Yoseloff Ltd.
123 New Bond Street
London, W.1, England

701.1
R74s


45123
July, 1963

Printed in the United States of America

# Preface

LIONELLO VENTURI IN THE INTRODUCTION TO HIS EXHAUSTIVE AND STILL outstanding *History of Art Criticism* (tr. Marriott, New York, 1936) paints a sorry picture of current understanding of the arts and their history. "If you say to a professor of art history," he asserts, "that his lessons are entirely without judgment, he will be offended. But if you ask him what are the standards of his judgments, he will reply that he sticks to the facts, that art is felt or not felt; or he will improvise some scheme used as a standard of appreciation," and he mentions a few, the inadequacy of which demonstrates in his opinion that the professor's "culture, unquestioned in all that concerns the documentation of the facts, shows some ignorance of all that refers to the ideas."

He skillfully exposes many weaknesses among past attempts to understand art, but clear evidence that any constructive understanding of his own has triumphed over these evils is rather hard to find. A long quotation, approvingly cited from the writings of Benedetto Croce supporting the value of art history as an aid to aesthetic criticism, is vague as

5

to the manner in which the two are related. Croce concludes that "the problem [of what historical facts are significant], determined case by case is only resolved case by case." Although this may be true in some degree if the aim of the history of art is to recognize "the moment in which taste is identified with art by the force of genius," as Venturi maintains at the end of his book, I feel sure that there is much valuable experience to be gained from the history of art at less dizzying heights. However, to achieve these modest and practical ends, and perhaps even in preparation for the rarefied perfection sought by Venturi and Croce, it is necessary to establish some reliable elementary guidance for the initial stages of artistic experience.

The most drastic need is an adequate interpretation of style that will establish direct connections between the forms of artistic expression and the patterns of human life in an orderly, objective and scientific fashion. A number of writers have noted a recurrent difference among the styles of the past between works of tactile and optic appeal, between styles showing classical or baroque predilections. Each has found his own terminology for this polarity, but it is nowhere so fully or aptly described as in the work of the late Heinrich Wölfflin. His eminence as an art historian has been widely acknowledged, yet his great contribution has done little to produce orderly thinking about the analysis of style. This is of course due in part to the fact that orderly thinking is not an important objective of most writers on art, especially those who deal with interpretation or "appreciation." But it is due in part also to Wölfflin's failure to discover significant motivation for the tendencies he so skillfully analyzed.

John Dewey observed in his important work on *Art as Experience* that "underneath the rhythm of every art and every work of art, there lies, as a substratum in the depths of the subconsciousness, the basic pattern of the relations of the live creature to his environment." In consonance with this suggestion, Wölfflin's inadequate explanation that the evolution of style is due to a change in the "mode of seeing," must be replaced by the observation that it is due to a change in the "mode of doing" both of the artist and his sponsoring society. Since even the slightest human gesture, like walking, vocal inflection, or the way a man snaps the brim of his hat, vividly conveys some aspect of personality, it cannot be doubted that so complex a gesture as the creative craftsmanship that goes into a work of art is richly freighted with human meaning.

To discover the means of interpreting style as the gesture of human and social personality is to open a broad channel of social and cultural inference arising directly from the quality of form in artistic creations. In the following pages, using some of the great advances that have recently been made in the understanding of human personality, I shall attempt to establish principles on which such illumination of the history of art may be based.

# Contents

# Plates

13

# STYLE IN ART

STYLE IN ART

# 1

# Introduction

TWO IMPORTANT PRINCIPLES HAVE EMERGED WITHIN THE PAST FIFTY OR one hundred years, one in the field of the social sciences generally, the other in the special area of the fine arts, that have not as yet been adequately recognized in cultural criticism or the analysis of style in the plastic arts. The first is that despite the tremendous accent on individual rights and capacities that are basic in modern life of the Western world, the social sciences have come to recognize that all individuals perform in response to certain common conditions of their natural or social environment. It is no longer believed to any great extent that human history has been formulated by the will of individual geniuses or potentates, but rather the opposite. Such individuals simply epitomize a strong common interest, which they perhaps more clearly read than others, and are better able to concretize for them in practical terms, thus being enabled to assume a leading role in its quest. This is true also of artists, however original their expression may seem to be.

19

The distinction between form and content is the second principle that has long been recognized, in addition to the expressive quality of form which reinforces the message of its content at a deeper level of consciousness. A most obvious example is found in the medium of music, where a slow or rapid beat, a particular key or harmony produces an immediate emotional response. The capacity of aesthetic form to create substantial human experience became so evident about three centuries ago, when instrumental accompaniments for great court masques were elaborated to the point where they could be performed significantly without the verbal content they were originally created to support, that it became the practice to compose music lacking any verbal references whatsoever. Architecture also conveys certain clear feelings, most noticeable at first in monumental assertions of human or divine power, that are due entirely to the quality of the forms employed and the manner of their disposition. The practice of painting and sculpture has been related throughout a long history of monumental creation to concrete visual associations. Emphasis on the quality of form in these mediums has been carried to the extreme lately, however, at which many people insist on the advantage of *eliminating* all pictorially recognizable reference to the objective world.

Influenced perhaps by this growth of emphasis on pure form in creative practice, art historians have effectively separated form and content in considerations of the art of the past, and the history of the plastic arts is now widely understood as essentially an evolution of style. Likewise, critics and scholars have conscientiously explored the contemporary historical circumstances related to their various fields of concentration, considerably illuminating the social significance of the great styles of the past. As yet, however, no attempt has been made to describe the *dynamics* of the relation between style in art and the social circumstances which it so plausibly epitomizes. How is it that the great social developments, the ideals of the palace, the temple or the market place guide the hand of the artist in his workshop? Patrons capable of any degree of precision in ordering monuments to their purpose have been few. Even in the most sophisticated eras, any prescription of the forms the artist had to produce can only have been specified by reference to previous forms, and all basic originality must have come from the artist, with his superior, specialized sensitivity to the expressive resources of his own medium.

EXPRESSIVE ROLE OF THE ARTIST

Just as the truly creative leaders who emerge in public affairs are those best equipped to realize the aims and interests of their times, those who become artists must also be profoundly sensitive to basic social forces. For the quality of form in their creations is related to the philosophy or emotional attitudes that result from general conditions of the life of their time. Of course it must not be supposed that there are systems of algebraic or symbolic formulae relating art to life, that can be coded and decoded intellectually, or even that a particular artist might be so conscious of a social responsibility along these lines that he would sit before his easel soliloquizing, "I have just read Martin Luther's momentous tract that he so dramatically fastened to the door of the castle church in Wittenberg (or the Declaration of Independence, or Newton's law of falling bodies) and I am sure it has great significance for our time. Now, how can I say the same thing, or present its motivating spirit, or underline its importance here on my canvas?" Few if any great artists have seen themselves in quite so responsible a role. Shakespeare and the Savoyard team alike thought they were composing potboilers. Rubens obviously painted his great series on the life of Marie de Medicis (Plate 41) to exploit her vanity in support of a diplomatic coup. Only some of the tortured characters immured in artists' colonies feel the crushing responsibility of creation as a universal service. The truly creative artist is a man of purposeful action—an agonist, not an agonizer.

Consciously, the true artist is concerned with no more than the immediate, practical aspects of his creative problem, though he is motivated at a deeper level by the same impulses that produce the outstanding social developments of his time. He moves ahead with the solution of a largely familiar practical problem, choosing without hesitation appropriate alternatives among the various phases of his craft, feeling, "Of course any person in his right mind would do this, and then thus, and then so!" The resultant expression is so complete and direct that the like-minded beholder will simply say, "Yes, this is my world," with a satisfaction as full and spontaneous or perhaps as fervent, but as uncritical as taking a deep breath or leaning back in a comfortable chair, as a cheer, a prayer or a "good cry."

Therefore, to understand a work of art, it is necessary to see the creative process as a succession of phases in each of which the artist makes a simple, spontaneous choice. Shall the description of the forms, for example, be accomplished by means of line or tone; shall the construction of space be accomplished by means of plane or recession; shall color be used for brightness or harmony? and so on. None of these alternatives are particularly complex or esoteric in themselves. Proposed independently, they present no difficulty to any sensitive individual in determining a clear preference based on subconscious inclinations little more obscure than the impulses of the artist. It is only in superimposing one choice on another, and blending all into skilled action that the artist brings a work of art to the complex individuality that makes it seem so inscrutable to the casual observer. Seeing the creative process in this way clarifies the apparent paradox of the potentially universal appeal of art, at the same time maintaining its dignity as a superior order of human activity and accounting for a certain degree of inaccessibility to general understanding.

In the analysis of such choices that is to follow, it will be apparent that the alternatives are related in *two major groupings,* one or the other of which a given artist, a given period or a given culture will tend to follow with a certain consistency. These basic categories of style in art, already quite widely recognized under a variety of designations paralleling the classic-baroque polarity, are associated with two basically opposite types of human conduct, motivated by diametrical interpretations of human experience, which will be described in the pages immediately following. Then the various aspects of form in the plastic arts will be described as they adhere to or express the basic attitudes; and finally the pertinence of the respective categories to patterns of historical evolution and social motivation will be explored.

Perhaps the most important requirement for adequate relation of the opposite classes of form and the patterns of human conduct whereby they are produced, with philosophical and emotional attitudes toward life throughout the past ages, but especially in modern times, is to recognize the basic importance of the dichotomy of all human feelings and emotions in respect to the functions of *producer* and *consumer.* The extent of concern with these functions in the life of an individual, their respective predominance among the interests of a community or an age, will produce highly characteristic patterns of practicality or sophistication, humanism or mysticism, intelligence or sensibility. Furthermore, as a carpenter or a scientist may be quite conscious of sensuous preferences in the food he eats or the clothes he wears, and the nineteenth-century gentleman may pursue a career in science, politics or agriculture, so a Golden Age may combine structural breadth and solidity with sensuous glory as in the style of a Titian. The constantly varying degrees in which these opposite functions motivate any given individual or age produce an infinite range of attitude corresponding profoundly with the evolution of human life. The relation of producing and consuming roles to stylistic expression in art cannot properly be discussed, however, until the formal categories of style have been adequately presented.

### APPEARANCE OF ORDER AND MYSTERY IN NATURAL ENVIRONMENT

Though there have been proposals that mankind has received supernatural or divine tutelage, in the struggle with his natural environment and the guidance of his social life, such as the Decalogue or the gift of fire stolen from the gods by Prometheus, there is a growing tendency to believe that the human race has developed an understanding of its environment predominantly from the accumulated experience of constant and necessary efforts to control it. Men function along the lines they have found to be effective. In a strange situation they tend to follow a pattern inspired by successes in previous encounters with seemingly similar situations. Master patterns governing an approach to all problems gradually develop and eventuate in general religious or philosophical guidance and cosmological interpretation.

*An important basic aspect of any such master pattern is whether it prescribes respect for order and the use of human powers of logical analysis; or whether instead, it relies upon striving more fortuitously and intuitively toward a given end.* Since virtually the beginning of his conscious life on earth, man has been faced with two opposite notions of his relation to the natural universe that surrounded him: Was it friend or foe? Of natural growth were the things he ate, and that gave him shelter. Of natural origin, too, were the beasts and meteorologic cataclysms that repeatedly threatened his existence. Searching for means to promote nature's friendly aspects, man's nascent intelligence began to recognize some of the more obvious manifestations of order in natural processes—unsupported objects fall, daytime and the seasons periodically return, and there is always a similar result from striking certain types of stone together. But because of his inability immediately to discern the full extent and precise nature of orderly relations in his environment, the value of the observations was limited and recourse to supernatural means and explanations constantly suggested itself. In fact it could hardly have been before the stage of neolithic community culture that his practical accomplishments began to have any marked effect on man's predominant feelings about his cosmic status.

C. G. Jung in a chapter on Archaic Man in his book, *Man in Search of a Soul,* discusses at some length the difficulty the primitive mind has in understanding the order of the natural universe, or in imagining any possibility of reliable control. Observations of the mystical attitudes of contemporary African tribes are noted, and he cites the belief even of a white Afrikander that man survives only by chance and with the greatest insecurity in the wilderness, which he felt "belonged to the animals, plants and microbes." Jung also contrasts graphically the rational European interpretation of environment through observation of events which follow in some apparent, causative sequence, discounting others as mere chance; with the mystical primitive attempt to interpret environment by a logic concerned only with *irregular* events (attributed to the sorcery of human or supernatural adversaries), discounting familiar occurrences as safe and needing no special attention. This example is cited to establish the plausibility of cosmological interpretations that do not follow rational patterns of cause and effect accepted by the Western world today, which indeed gives little more than lip service to the rule of reason in many other fields.

Following aeons of physical evolution, man at the dawn of human culture found himself equipped with a highly efficient apparatus for receiving sensory impressions of his environment, to which he reacted instinctively or reflexively, like any other animal. He completely lacked, however, any means of understanding them. In his remarkable series of essays under the title of *The Immense Journey,* anthropologist Loren Eiseley presents the evolutionary mystery of how the sudden emergence of the human brain could possibly have taken place in a process explained only by the doctrine of natural selection. Perhaps related, certainly equally mysterious, is the explanation of why men ever embarked on the lengthy, tortuous and frequently disastrous business of equipping themselves to understand what was going on about them.

At first, hitherto undifferentiated sensory phenomena must have seemed somehow connected, or certain long-sensed relations, reflexive associations, may have assumed a new and distinct importance. When connections appeared *among the connections,* it may be said that the sense of logic or order was born. "If this is true, then that may also follow. . . . My impulse is to do thus and so, but have I observed anything that might serve to redirect that impulse more effectively?" Eventually such reflections were constellated into an embracing, proto-philosophical or religious pattern indicating that the universe had a particular character relative to the interests and purposes of mankind as a special order of being.

Throughout this immeasurable period of development, reflected only in its very final stages by the remains of prehistoric culture, man never felt fully in control of his natural environment, and the relative importance or accessibility of any basic pattern of order remained fluid and incomplete. Even when the tenuous security of the neolithic settlement generated some awareness of his distinction from other forms of life, it is not to be supposed that the primitive artist functioned with any consciousness of the opposite beliefs regarding the depth of order in the universe, like an office seeker advocating a particular political program, or a convert renouncing his past for a revelation of divine truth. Primitive artists, whose singing, dancing, painting, or carving suggested a belief in an orderly universe, celebrated a faith in human power even though for all practical purposes their professions were more of a prayer than a reliably accepted fact. In the earlier stages, their artistic creations continually implored, glorified, or attempted to repel the unfathomable powers behind the complexity of nature they felt to be utterly impenetrable, although there was nothing but their faith to substantiate the efficacy of any of their practices. John Dewey says (*Art as Experience,* p. 29), "Only those who are so far removed from the earlier experiences as to miss their sense will conclude that rites and ceremonies were merely technical devices for securing rain, sons, crops, success in battle. Of course they had this magical intent, but they were enduringly enacted, we may be sure, in spite of all practical failures, because they were immediate enhancements of the experience of living."

Cultural expression can thus be seen in a sense as the exercise of accepted conventionalities in a man-made precinct where immunity from interference by unreasonable forces of nature permitted formal consummation of the desired end without embarrassment or disaster—a kind of laboratory demonstration with antipractical rather than practical controls. In the hunting dance a horned figure, of far more terrifying aspect than a natural bison, roars and plunges at the human hunters, who are prepared with a formula of shouts and gestures that cannot fail eventually to bring him to defeat. There is no question about the outcome of the ceremonial combat, nor is there much question either in the minds of those who must go forth and face the actual beast in the field next day, that he will be every bit as ferocious as ever; but the elation and group support experienced in the ceremonial triumph dull the memory of earlier casualties of the hunt, making the chances of survival seem greater, while the focal concern of the dependent community ennobles the danger of the hunters and gives the others some sense of participation.

## MANKIND'S ANALYTICAL AND INTUITIVE RESPONSES

Of course all primitive people were fearful of natural environment to some extent, just as most people today are beset by anxieties about their social environment. The important cultural distinction is between those who tend to cast away all reliance upon human capacity and think only of abject or profligate appeal to a mysterious power, be it some primitive Astarte or a modern "Lady Luck," as against those who gradually came to see the human creature superior to all others on earth, recognizing his ability to establish some degree of control through his own distinct powers based on logical or analytical understanding. It may not always be easy to distinguish those in more advanced societies who strive to meet the problems of survival by self-reliant, reasoned analysis. Today everyone gives lip service to the dignity of man and the efficiency of human intelligence, without always realizing that the one is not the same as personal pretension, nor the other a problemless Nirvana guaranteed by intellectual or economic conjuration.

Presumably no prehistoric culture achieved a complete sense of man's centrality, security, or control in the natural world. Had they, they might have felt sufficiently important to have created historical records. In fact, it was ages before the earliest men even felt any distinction whatever from their natural surroundings. The naturalistic art of early (paleolithic) nomadic hunters, such as the cave paintings first seen at Altamira, Spain or Lascaux in France (Plate 1a) attempts a visual counterfeit of the animals of the hunt, upon which men were dependent for survival. Great emotional tension is therefore involved. How to ensure the presence and discovery of the herds? How to enhance the fleetness and skill of the hunters to achieve success in the chase? The quite skillful images are generally found in deep, unlit caves which were uninhabitable and to which men must have resorted only for ceremonial purposes. Often there are many drawings on a wall with no compositional relation, as though they were devotionally created on many repeated occasions in a place presumed auspicious. The endeavor to follow the appearance of the crucial natural object as closely as possible, with no attempt to change or compose it according to aesthetic preference of the human psyche, expresses man's submission to the impenetrable mystery of nature.

On the other hand, the abstract geometrical art that developed in the neolithic period, deriving from the manually fashioned surfaces of craft objects, as in the art of the American Indian (Plate 1b) represents a realization that human intelligence is capable of exerting its will to some extent against natural forces and contriving for itself a relative degree of comfort and security. Few precisely geometrical forms in nature are apparent to unaided human vision, yet all but the most sophisticated products of man's hand are highly dependent on the square, the circle and the triangle.

W. Worringer, in *Form Problems of the Gothic,* under a discussion of Primitive Man (tr. John Shapley, New York, n.d., p. 31), was among the first to recognize that primitive art profoundly conveyed the feelings of its creators, and stated, ". . . because of the relationship of fear in which primitive man stands to the phenomenal world, the most urgent need of his mind and soul must be to press forward to invariables, which save him from the chaotic confusions of mind and sense." However, in his statements that geometric abstraction was created as a "table of symbolic invariables," and that "primitive ornament is conjuration to dispel that horror of the incoherent surrounding world . . ." it is not clear whether he has noted how practical and substantial was the power his "invariables" possessed to dispel horror, since it was derived from the very real basis of their origin in the manual crafts.

The first real relief mankind can have felt from the constant terror of natural catastrophe was made possible within the community by the discovery of agricultural techniques that obviated the necessity of constant or frequent migration. To find that human logic and will could direct nature to the extent of producing a fairly reliable localized supply of food in the cultivation of crops and domestication of cattle was in itself a tremendous step. Moreover, it gave rise to a series of successes in other areas of environmental control that had vast cultural consequences. Dwellings were created for personal protection, which was increased by grouping or even stockading them in defensive fashion. For the storage of food, vessels came to be created out of wood, clay, and basketry, the last named also giving rise to the weaving of textiles. The primitive savage literally became a "new man" (or perhaps now at last a "man" culturally as well as physiologically) and felt the change every time he stepped within the precincts of his tiny haven from the surrounding wilderness.

The essence of craft procedures is *logic* in the sense of causative sequence, and *regularity* is an obvious corollary. The mark of hand or tool, the interval of the stroke, the spacing of weft or coil, are bound to be consistent and rhythmical. As the hunter, the warrior, the messenger, or even the field hand, enters the village and steps into his own hut, the terrors of the storm, the lurking beast, or the human enemy are almost completely dispelled. He is able to relax, to expand emotionally in reflection or creative activity and the association of affectionate human contacts. The aesthetic or formal quality associated with this nourishing experience is the rhythmic, quasi-geometrical clarity resulting from the practical regularity of craft processes and diametrically opposed to the tumultuous, undisciplined irregularity of natural growth. It soon becomes the aim of the craftsman to enhance this human distinction of his product in every possible way. The potter's thumbprints or the metal smith's hammer marks are formalized into rounds and bosses; parallel striations reflect the clay coils of built-up pottery or the tool marks of later work from the wheel; the chevron, diaper, meander and other rectilinear patterns derive from the weaving of baskets and cloth. This is the more complete significance of the abstract, geometrical vocabulary of neolithic decoration, rather a *celebration* of human power over nature than simply the "conjuration" Worringer saw.

Curiously enough, when that celebration becomes at length devoid of terror, when it evolves into a completely human or anthropocentric faith, cultural expression returns to naturalistic representation, but with a clarified, analytical handling of form. Thereafter a tendency toward a *somewhat* cyclical recurrence of the opposite types of style (which will be called respectively "analytical" and "sensational") may be noted in the evolution of cultural expression. Within a given culture the analytical always precedes the sensational; for example, in Greece archaic and fifth-century clarity gives way to Hellenistic profusion, and style in Italy later follows a similar sequence from the proto-Renaissance through the high Renaissance or Golden Age to the Baroque.

This pattern, which will be subject to detailed examination later, does not begin until Greek civilization produces a completely anthropocentric philosophy, and Western society becomes virtually a continuous growth. Up to that time, although human power over environment had grown vastly, the threat of natural catastrophe in Western Europe remained a factor in cultural formulations; the natural world continued to be conceived as motivated by an independent if not necessarily antagonistic will, and the Greek view was impossible. Comprehensive long-range patterns did not occur because the growth of the prehistoric community was not a continuous process, often involving conflicts in which one side or the other was either annihilated or enslaved, and cultural beginnings were frequently wiped out in other ways. Though the human record since history began is marred on every page with deeds of hideous violence, they seem not to have produced such complete breaks in the continuity of social organization, production, and culture as were characteristic of prehistoric struggle. Unlike the isolated early tribal groups, opposing forces since about the beginning of historical times have borne sufficient relation to one another that change constituted rather a shifting of power from one force in human society to another. Violence was merely an incidental concomitant with little direct influence on the social structure, regardless of how much material wealth and human life it managed to destroy.

Influences remained even from the pre-hellenic Aegaean civilizations, the Etruscans, and the barbaric cultures of northern Europe, upon the styles of their conquerors, but the supplanting cultures were essentially new and independent. Since the empires of Greece and Rome, however, changes in social organization have been predominantly evolutionary, and the new artistic expressions have been accomplished gradually within an unbroken craft tradition, the later artists adapting familiar forms and materials to the new objectives of cultural expression. The exception, of course, is the conquest of the Western Hemisphere by Europeans, who virtually extinguished the cultures they found there.

Competing throughout the early stages of man's attempts to understand and develop his relation to his natural environment were the two opposite views of natural motivation, and the respectively analytical and sensational moods to which they gave rise. With some interaction, these have persisted to the present, characterizing the reactions of various societies to the particular environments, human as well as natural, in which they have functioned. Beliefs in fundamentally rational, or on the other hand mystical, motivation of the universe have given rise to basically opposite ways of living throughout the entire range of human culture. Facing a given problem, a man must decide whether or not he can solve it by deductions from his previous experience, according to some general patterns of logical understanding to which his community subscribes. Without sufficient faith in the adequacy of human resources, he must grope for some contact with those mysterious forces, unknown but deeply presumed, that seem to order the universe beyond the limits of his own effectiveness. These procedures might be called respectively "analytical" and "sensational." Under the former, recourse is taken to generalized observations relative to the problems in hand, or the invention of logical presumptions, and requires a confident respect for human capacities which eventuates in humanistic culture and anthropocentric philosophy. The "sensational" attitude demonstrates a lack of faith in logical human interpretation of environmental forces, and causes a persistent, anxious attention to the variety and complexity of specific natural phenomena, to be dealt with by conjectural or revelatory prescriptions.

An artist with an analytical attitude would not attempt a complete visual counterfeit of the factors in his environment to which the particular work of art had reference, but would re-create his subject out of component elements to which its natural complexity had been reduced by human logic. The result might not seem very close to the visual *appearance* of nature, but would embody the essence of reality most significant for human understanding. A clear example is the work of fifteenth-century artists in Western Europe, who were penetrating and exact in their exposition of reality, yet have been frequently depreciated as naïve and primitive by the sensational bias of subsequent criticism.

The creative person who follows a sensational procedure of cultural expression, with no inclination to see or depend on a logical pattern in experience, would be forced either (1) to attempt a counterfeit of full natural complexity; (2) to summarize it intuitively; or (3) to turn his back on natural appearance entirely and indulge his aesthetic or emotional fantasies. Since all of these depend on creation of sensations no more clarified than they are in natural experience, they demonstrate a preference which might be called "sensational" on the part of the artist—a sensuous, intuitive acceptance of or submission to his environment, rather than the dissecting probe of analytical expression.

Other terms which might be used to describe the psychological or philosophical polarity that motivates style in art are noumenal and phenomenal, or conceptual and intuitive. Curt Sachs uses the Greek words *ethos* and *pathos* in *The Commonwealth of Art,* and many more could be found. The terms "analytical" and "sensational" are used here as seemingly most applicable to plastic experience.

## LOGICAL AND SPONTANEOUS TENDENCIES OF HUMAN PERSONALITY

An apparent digression at this point may further clarify the nature of the two attitudes toward human environment that basically govern differences in cultural expression. For the opposite attitudes of logical or intuitive approach to life are still basic and prevalent today, no longer motivated primarily by the struggle with natural environment, but by personal experience with the embracing society. Whereas in the perspective of the past, when the rhythms of cultural evolution were so much more gradual, these attitudes seem to characterize an entire period or race (doubtless to some extent an oversimplification), today the opposites can be encountered on all sides.

A scholar may find the office of one respected colleague a wealth of apparent confusion; his writings abstruse, wandering; his personality volatile, perhaps charming, but unpredictable. Another, no more or less capable in point of results, will inhabit an office in which notes, correspondence, classroom exercises are all neatly arranged and readily recognizable; his speech and writing moves logically from premise to conclusion. Charm is not the word often associated with him, but he is dependable, helpful in developing the ideas of his associates, for he listens impersonally, analytically.

Similar differences are found even in the sphere of highly practical industrial operations. A mechanic approaching the bench of a shopmate, perhaps to borrow a tool, finds a chaotic assortment. His friend paws about for a moment among the dozen or so tools already out, or in the incredibly jumbled drawers of his toolbox, and comes up with the requested item soon enough to make it evident that he knew pretty much where it was. Yet another, no better nor worse in his ability to produce, will hardly set a tool down on his bench, but will have a rack where it goes back regularly to an appointed place. Anyone could find a tool in his box within a few seconds because the arrangement is so clear.

There is the person who enters a room coming home from a round of errands, dropping clothing and bundles helter-skelter—not the "spoiled" type who expects them to be picked up by someone else, but one who simply does things that way. In a moment they will all be put away in a flurry of "housekeeping." But there are others who step to the kitchen door with the bundle of groceries, drop the books on the library table, and reach into the hall closet for a hanger before their other hand is out of the overcoat.

In such fundamentally different modes of living, directed nonetheless toward the same aims and by the same customs, may be read opposite feelings about the orderliness of environment and events. Of course it is no longer the struggle with elemental nature that impresses a sense of inadequacy, insecurity or stress on human personality, individually and in groups. Perhaps it might be said to be the struggle with "*human nature,*" or social environment that is the predominant influence today. Following a general description of the manner in which these impulses can be read from an analysis of style in art, some of the major influences which blend to produce the faith of the individual in any given culture will be described.

All of human personality and consequently all of human culture can be analyzed significantly in respect to the extremes of faith in order, favoring analysis, calculation and the joys of security and dependable knowledge; or a lack of faith in order, inspiring resort to intuition, impulse and the joys or excitement of mystery and sensation. In primitive culture the dichotomy was virtually complete and these attitudes were mutually exclusive on the cultural level. As society evolved, the discovered patterns of order became more complex and inescapable, the direction of intuition more and more intelligent; imagination aided the further discovery of order, until a closer balance was achieved between induction and deduction in the most effective thought.

It may even be said that modern scientific method represents a *complete faith* in order applied to the *full complexity* of the natural and social cosmos. The initial antagonism has at last been completely eliminated in the philosophies behind the most advanced modern practice, except for individual differences of emotional preference which will probably remain forever at some irreducible minimum. Conceivably, however, much current misunderstanding throughout the world may be reduced as the two philosophical extremes are amalgamated in other fields which are now governed by emotion and prejudice, as they have been so successfully combined in the field of the natural sciences. The requirement that thought be orderly and the belief that orderly analysis must guide intuition even in solving the most subtle or complex problems is already so extensively taken for granted, that a special effort must be made to understand those periods in which one or the other extreme dominated the whole pattern of human conduct. Yet the scientific method is really very young (discounting some early, sporadic appearances) and has still to be extended to considerable areas of human thought.

# 2

# Stylistically Significant Aspects of Form

GIVEN THE TENDENCY OF ALL HUMAN THOUGHT AND FEELING TOWARD either orderly, analytical techniques or mystical, intuitive exercises for the control of environment by contact with dominant cosmic influences, what will be the appearance of these alternatives in plastic expression? The task of the painter, sculptor, or architect is to create forms that will develop a given environment for a particular purpose, in terms of the aims and beliefs of the society of which he is a part. He does not convey these beliefs simply by creating a conventional, recognizable image of Zeus or Buddha or Christ or a wealthy merchant prince, but also by the form in which these images are cast. A Christ from a Byzantine mosaic or an Hiberno-Saxon manuscript illumination can hardly be recognized as the same character that is represented in a rococo Transfiguration or a Renaissance Crucifixion. There is not only a change of role from Just Judge and Creator (Plate 34b) to Man of Sorrows, but also a change in the manner in which the forms themselves are created. The differences in form become even more significant, perhaps, when the scriptural inter-

34

pretation is fairly close, and a Man of Sorrows by Mantegna (Plate 2a) for example, is contrasted with a later figure by Caracci (Plate 2b).

Unfortunately, examination of the plastic arts in the past has failed adequately to separate form and content in the analysis of style. Attempts to concentrate on the formal aspect without a clear procedure for distinguishing it, in view of the predominantly subjective methods of latter-day criticism, have led right back to content. Known cultural attitudes are read into the form, such as the "intellectual" quality of Renaissance style, and the "emotional" quality of the Baroque and Rococo periods. This sort of thing can lead to such contradictions as too glibly equating the "dynamic" quality of an eighteenth-century boudoir piece with the gaiety of French court life. For is not the "dynamic quality" in Gothic religious architecture supposed to express the heaven-tending zeal of truly believing godliness? Adequate explanation for such paradoxical terminology requires the construction of a system more complex than can be expected to arise spontaneously in the subjective reactions of any particular critic. Moreover, this system should account for the *process* whereby a given emotional or philosophical attitude may impress itself on the material of the arts.

Despite the undeniable complexity of cultural expression, an analytical procedure answering both of these requirements may be constructed upon the recognition of the two basic attitudes toward interpretation of human experience already cited. It is possible by examining the various aspects of plastic creation—form, space, enframement, composition, etc.—on the basis of alternatively analytical and sensational interpretations of the universe and the resulting procedures in human conduct, to discover opposite approaches to each aspect of form establishing two major categories of style.

### LINE AND TONE

Linear description of form in art is clearly the analytical tendency to deal with the creative problem by precise definition of component parts. Actually lines do not exist in nature. Edges exist and sometimes look like lines, but if the beholder moves a step to the left or right as he looks at a cylindrical shape, the vertical edge is at a new point of the circle, and of course there is no longer a line where the old edge was. The nearest thing to a line in the field of human sensations has no reference to the retina but to the hand. It is a gesture around the form. Hence a linear presentation might be said to represent the *tactile* reality of a form rather than its *optic* appearance, with the term "tactile" of course referring to the entire sense of bulk or shape rather than mere surface quality. Some indication of light and shade is admissible, as in the style of Leonardo da Vinci or even of earlier fifteenth-century Italian painters (Plate 21b). The criterion is constant clarity of the edges of the form, resulting in a primary sensation of particular shapes rather than of a generally patterned surface arousing optical *associations* with shapes.

As lines do not exist in nature (except as very narrow planes or as markings, but not as edges or contours) so edges are often actually invisible, as on the dark side of an object next to the cast shadow, or on limbs beneath drapery. For the artist to reconstruct, emphasize or indicate these edges is to analyze and complete appearances by reference to his own knowledge and logic in the interest of a clear, generalized picture of the universe. The light on this tree or desk gives it one appearance today, another tomorrow. Such a history is chaotic, practical reference to any part misleading. A faith in order demands elimination of the momentary, the accidental, to discover the permanent, general, practical truth. The utmost in practical description, which is precise enough to enable a craftsman to create the intended object, is of course a "blueprint" or mechanical drawing in which all edges are simply lines, undistorted by *any* reference to human vision.

The light and shade on an object obviously produces a retinal sensation which may or may not adequately convey a sense of the shape that really exists. Gradually, by constant association, the human mind and motor controls achieve so high a degree of ability to recognize objects from the retinal images that the necessity of translation is forgotten, but occasional confusions indicate the process is not perfect. In cultural expression, however, the artist may modify any phase of the visual image, so that attention is directed toward the dramatic quality of exaggerated contrasts of light and shade (chiaroscuro), the charm of brilliant illumination, or the range of color sensations to the point of seriously hindering a precise apprehension of shape and structure. Hence the *expression* when light and shade (or tone) primarily is used for description instead of line, is one of accident, impermanence, specific and therefore apractical observation—in varying degrees to be sure, as of Vermeer on the one hand or of Hals, El Greco, Monticelli or Monet on the other. The difference in feeling between tactile and optic treatments of form is clearly indicated by comparison of an engraving called *Battle of the*

*Ten Nudes* by the fifteenth-century Florentine artist Antonio Pollaiuolo, with an etching of a nude male model by Rembrandt (Plate 3a and
b). Even though the later artist is using a technique based on lines, he
masses them into tones to produce an optic effect; whereas the earlier
Italian, although he shows an awareness of the possibility of using lines
to compose tones, nevertheless produces a strongly linear effect.

Since the values in tonal description of form pertain directly to
visual sensation, works in this style might be termed "optic," to indicate
their emphasis on the retinal sensations of light and shade. Historically,
optical realization of form has presented two major phases. The first is
*illusionistic,* in which representation of the objective world is still the
major aim of the artist, but an optic type of realism is preferred either
because of the immediate sense of specific reality it conveys, or for the
excitingly accidental and aesthetically ingratiating qualities of tone as
opposed to line (Plate 39 and 40b). Following this a *postillusionistic*
stage may develop, when the patrons of art lose all concern with objective
reality, and require the artist simply to use the elements of his medium
abstractly, to create an artificial experience out of purely emotional or
aesthetic material. The plastic arts in the twentieth century have been
dominated by a postillusionistic form of sensational style in which the
fantasy of the artist is paramount (Plate 42). Expressionism, Dadaism and
surrealism represent phases of emotional expression, whereas most post-
impressionist artists and subsequent abstract movements to nonobjectiv-
ism clearly represent the growth of interest in predominantly aesthetic
content.

### PLANE AND RECESSION

In much early art, even as sophisticated as actively realistic Greek
vase painting and architectural relief sculpture of the fifth century B.C.
(Plate 4a), there is no attempt to present any illusion of space whatsoever;
the objects represented are felt to exist on the surface of the decorated
object or plane rather than in an independent picture space. When the
prevailing trend toward visual reality in Western art encompassed the
illusion of a spatial setting, two opposite ways of presenting space were
developed. Reference to deep space has been created in works of art
either by establishment of successive *planes* of depth, or a continuous
*recession* of objects and movement.

Planimetric construction of space is clearly a logical process. An artist familiar with the appearance of diminution in distant objects thinks: Objects are near, far and in between. I place my important objects at the picture plane, distant objects at the horizon, and the rest in the middle distance. These are three precise categories of depth, and three precise planes result. This is an analytical process that avoids the obscuring of shapes by excessive overlapping of one object on another, and presents that very orderly appearance in the spatially regimented distribution of objects which is so characteristic of fifteenth-century painting (Plate 12a). Early landscape painting of the Renaissance in Venice avoids the unnatural appearance of regimentation by superimposing a pattern of light and dark areas, but the planimetric construction of deep space remains basic.

Nature, however, does not afford human vision the convenience of lining up her forms in deferential ranks. The actual *sensation* of objects in depth is of an infinite series receding in any given direction, as the attention of the spectator turns this way or that. Recessional association of objects in a work of art to suggest their existence in depth therefore belongs to the sensational category. It is served by the system of "angular" or "two point" perspective, whereas "parallel" or "one point" perspective produces a planimetric construction of space.

Leonardo da Vinci's *Last Supper* and the *Peasant Wedding* by Breughel (Plate 5a and b) show two scenes arranged at a long table, the former planimetrically in parallel perspective, used incidentally to emphasize the figure of Christ by placing the single vanishing point behind His head so that all receding horizontal lines must point in that direction. Breughel, who is only a little later than Leonardo and still predominantly analytical, prefers a recessional arrangement because of the general affinity in the north for sensational aspects of style.

In the high Renaissance painting of the Venetian artist Tintoretto (Plate 12b), the recessional arrangement and movement are so insistent as to appear almost as regimented as earlier planimetric compositions. In some of his paintings it seems almost as if a fifteenth century composition were turned back about thirty degrees from the picture plane to create a sense of recessional movement which is not entirely illusionistic. Other high Renaissance and even later artists *combine* recessional movement or distribution of objects with a planimetric construction of the setting for a contrapuntal enhancement of the sense of space. Raphael's *School of Athens* (Plate 26) in the Vatican suggests a beginning of this approach, which achieves a very special quality in the seventeenth century Dutch painting of Vermeer (Plate 39a) and deHooch.

Recessional quality in spatial composition may refer not only to the illusion of depth, but also to the movement of objects toward and away from the picture or relief plane when little or no deep space is represented. In the development of the Italian Baroque style, this appears as early as Titian's *Entombment* (Plate 24b). This characteristic of the Hellenistic high relief sculpture of the gigantomachy from the Great Altar at Pergamon (Plate 4b) in which figures fill the entire area and no environment at all is represented, also serves to introduce a structural confusion in the design, typical of sensational style (see page 45 ff.). Such treatment eliminates from the composition any recognition of the solid, two dimensional surface on which the work is raised, substituting the illusion of a spatial volume in which the composition weaves backward and forward. This contradicts the structure and substance of the architectural design, making the weight above appear to be supported simply on a writhing mass of human bodies.

Early planimetric low relief emphasizes line and plane in the silhouetted reduction of volume often to a medallion-like thinness raised on the undisturbed surface, like the figures in Wedgewood china or the general type of design called "appliqué." The figures of Aphrodite and the two nymphs receiving her from the sea as represented in the early fifth century B.C. Greek altar (Plate 4a) are not reduced quite as much as figures on a coin, but their composition is governed by the plane of the surface on which they are raised and no sense of depth behind them is created. An intermediate approach is exemplified rather brilliantly in the well known horsemen of the Panathenaic Procession on the inner frieze of the Parthenon. The volume of the overlapping horses and their riders illusionistically contradicts the volume of the quite shallow relief, but their movement is held strictly within the plane of the cella wall on which they are carved, and no spatial environment is suggested.

Recessional movement and depth of composition is the attempt to imply with solid materials an immaterial something that cannot be seen or grasped except by association with the sensations of visual experience. Thus there is something sensational about any representation of space in art, which was not attempted at all in the earliest and most literally analytical stages. When representation of space became a necessary and familiar illusion, then distinct manners of achieving it arose that were variously analytical and sensational in respect to one another. This illustrates the generally comparative quality of terms in the polar categories. That is to say, while a painting in parallel perspective may be analytical as contrasted with a painting in angular perspective, all the illusionism of European art since the early fifteenth century is sensational as compared with preceding nonillusionistic styles. Or to put it another way, illusionism is itself sensational, but the problems it poses admit of respectively analytical or sensational solutions.

## CLOSED AND OPEN COMPOSITION

The essential unity which transforms a collection of sensations in the plastic arts into a work of art may be achieved (in part) either by firmly enclosing them within a frame or by attaching them radially to a firm focus. In the former case, though some emphasis may be conferred on a central figure, group or object of superior importance, attention is distributed with approximate uniformity throughout the area, stopping completely at the frame (Plate 23a). In a radial composition the focus must be powerfully developed to exert a controlling force. The material of the composition and the attention it will bear diminishes toward the periphery where it bevels down to nothing, like a vignette illustration of a book page. Though enframement and focus respectively define the compositional unity in these two aspects of style, it must be noted that the *presence* of a frame is not a decisive characteristic. For almost all paintings must be framed. However, the frame may or may not constitute a definitive enclosure of the material of the composition. In fact the complete peripheral diminution of a radial composition is almost never depicted in a framed painting. Radiation from the focus may set up a succession of forms or motion that *implies,* by association with visual experience, a continuity beyond the relatively accidental incidence of the frame (Plate 37b).

The paradox of a frame that does not enframe is made clearer by contrasting a theatrical production seen through a proscenium arch with the view from a window on a busy street. Everything that is part of the action of the play must somehow be actualized within that arch or it simply does not become part of the dramatic experience. Whether seen from left or right, front or rear, orchestra or balcony, the entire audience sees exactly the same play. To marshal the contents of a painting similarly in respect to a frame is obviously an analytical job involving resolution of the subject into its component parts, each of which must be produced.

But life seen through an open window is merely a fragment which differs radically in content or concentration as the spectator moves from one side of the room to another, closer or farther away. The branch hanging in the corner of the window implies a tree growing on the lawn. From another position the whole tree may be seen. The steaming radiator of a motor truck at the left implies its toilsome journey up the hill. Soon it is in the center of the scene and then it passes out of the picture on the right. An artist trying to tell a precise story by reference to the fluctuating continuity outside the window must contrive to select a moment and a position from which the apparently accidental coincidence of events or sensations will most effectively suggest the greater and more significant total. Involving a high degree of particularity as well as suggestion, this is obviously a sensational approach.

These opposite types of composition might be termed "closed" and "open." Closed form is as analytical as an inventory. "Here is what I am concerned with," says the artist, "no more, no less." There is a minimum of intuitive suggestion about forms, space, or movement continuing beyond the frame, all of which are generally stopped by terminal figures within the composition itself before the frame is reached. There is a sense of finality about what the picture is intended to include, as of a research into a given subject rather than an actual contact with it. Open form, on the other hand, may present the vividness of actuality in all its particular detail, but this is compensated for by the limitation that it can reveal only a passing moment. The continuum in time or space with which the specific reference is associated, and which in fact gives it meaning, is only implied. Obviously this dependence on specific observation is one way in which open form may be associated with other qualities of the sensational category (Plate 7b).

Open form involves not only weakening the authority of the frame, but also of the picture plane. The analogy of the stage again holds. In a closed composition the artist contrives to have his important actors constantly at the footlights. But in life it is not always so. An actual passer-by on the day that the Virgin was presented in the Temple, would find casual bystanders and other secondary figures nearest him, and would have to peer over their heads to see the child mounting the steps toward the high priest, just as in Tintoretto's noted painting of the event (Plate 12b). Thus in minimizing any precise or formal boundary between the spectator and the action of the composition, as well as the fluidity of the outer enframement, open form corresponds to the unbounded character of actual sight. Seventeenth- and eighteenth-century Italian mural painters, as in Tiepolo's Cleopatra series in the Palazzo Labia in Venice (Plate 6), so completely eliminated indications both of enframement and picture plane, that the space of the picture was absolutely continuous with the space of the room. It was the artist's intention to give the beholder the sensation, spatially at least, of actual presence at the depicted event.

Closed and open composition adds another pair of alternatives for the artist motivated either by an analytical or sensational view of nature and society. As in the others, his choice is not absolute, for between the extremes of a fifteenth-century Florentine painting and the Tiepolo murals there are blends like Raphael's *School of Athens* (Plate 26), clearly regimented but with the main figures quite removed from the picture plane, and several incomplete enframements within the composition. The thoroughly supported illusion of continuity between the mural and the space it bounds, as in the Tiepolos and earlier Baroque ceiling decorations, might seem to achieve the ultimate in open form. Actually, however, the *"coupd'oeil"* compositions of nineteenth-century French artists as in Degas' *Absinthe Drinkers* or *At the Races* (Plate 7b), are so fragmentary that in comparison the seventeenth- and eighteenth-century works might seem analytical in their completeness.

### MECHANICAL AND ORGANIC ARTICULATION

The tremendous mass of stimuli constantly presented to the human senses would give rise to paralyzing confusion were it not for the faculty of attention, which makes possible selection of centers for concentration. The function of the artist in an important degree is to present the senses with an experience in which the elements are pre-coordinated so perfectly that attention may grasp the whole, feeling power and expansion in a microcosm devoid of elusive irrelevancies. Every work of art involves thorough coordination of a quantity of sensory material, but there are two opposite ways in which the components may be related. The relation between the parts may be like the parts of a machine, which are always independent, replaceable, no matter how intricate the motion in which they participate. Or the parts may be related as in a living organism where one grows into another; they are interlocked in networks of veins and nerves, overlaid with intimately attached layers of fatty tissue and epidermis, so that extensive study of several phases of anatomy is necessary to understand the whole; skilled use of the scalpel is needed to dissect it; few parts can successfully be removed or replaced, and these only by the most subtle and skillful techniques.

Presenting the independent completeness of component parts in a work of art which obviously follows the proclivity of the human mind for logical analysis, may begin with the exhaustive description of detail. This is seen, for example, in the complete and uniform description of each unit in a piece of jewelry or textile pattern, however repetitive, as in an early Flemish portrait (Plate 8a). In fifteenth-century Italian painting, when anatomy was still a new and exciting subject for the "Naturalists," separate parts of the body were articulated to the limits of credibility, and a nude by Pollaiuolo or Verrocchio (Plates 3a and 21b) thereby acquires a bumpy appearance that is hardly pleasing except in terms of this powerful contemporary interest. The precise drawing of each joint in the fingers and toes of the Three Graces from Botticelli's *Primavera* (Plate 23b), exciting as it may be in its capacity for arousing rapid-fire tactile experience as the beholder's attention moves from part to part, detracts in some degree from the intended beauty of the figures seen *as a whole*. There is a minimum tendency to merge groups of people in this type of painting into the cohesive semblance of a crowd; they remain clearly a precise number of individuals (a group of bit players rather than a mob scene). Mechanical articulation is also associated with planimetric construction of space in which different ranges of depth are separated and overlapping of figures avoided; and linear description of form is virtually a necessity.

Organic articulation (the adjective referring to the quality of *natural* organisms) tends to merge the material presented into a continuous fabric by weakening or eliminating definitive outlines or other separation, and promoting interdependence of component parts. Thus anatomical or costume detail is often summarized in a few skillfully selected details, which can hardly be recognized in isolation (like the hand holding the brush in Velasquez's self-portrait from *Las Meniñas* (Plate 8b). Thus the detail cannot support any attention independent of or distracting from the total effect, and is itself dependent on its relation to the whole for its meaning. Groups of figures are merged into a crowd, with some represented mainly by a waving hand, others by just a head, a considerable number being implied with only a few fully visible figures represented. Such a group is frequently treated as a single object in an elaborate composition, contributing a unified major axis to the general movement, one spot of light or dark to the pattern of chiaroscuro, and so on. In this way the group acts as a kind of subassembly which helps control a quantity of detail, clearly subordinating its constituent minor figures to the emphatic central subject with which their total weight or area is approximately equated.

Throughout the picture, in fact, there will be a graded scale of emphasis and subordination, with full treatment given only to focal figures, the surrounding ones being developed with less and less attention as they are removed from the important centers. Obviously recessional space facilitates this unity and flow of attention; and tonal description of forms not only permits elimination of distinguishing outlines, but also provides an important means of emphasis by high illumination and full modeling, as well as subordination in shaded areas where minor figures are reduced to shadowy silhouettes.

Color is also an important means of effecting the articulation of a work of art. In academic discussions of the use of color, it is usual to indicate on a "color wheel" (which is the spectrum bent in a circle) that "complementary colors" fall in diametrical opposition, and from this to pronounce what colors may and may not be used together harmoniously, or to describe various harmonic relations of color. This often causes the student to ignore the fact that harmonious use of color is only one alternative. Color can be applied also, as it was in the fifteenth century generally throughout Western European art, in a series of bright, contrasting hues. This procedure, besides conferring a simple gaiety or brightness, also serves to differentiate one shape from another, as countries are colored differently on a map to clarify the limits of their extent. This separation by contrasting colors clearly contributes to a mechanical articulation of the composition in the plastic arts, whereas harmonious control of color adds a pattern of interdependence to reinforce the other devices for compositional fusion or organic continuity in a sensational style.

Although fusion of composition as a sophisticated quality tends to be considered superior by current prejudice, there are positive values also in the more mechanically articulated or discrete type of composition. In a sense, uniform emphasis throughout all parts of a composition may seem to weaken its coherence, but on the other hand it supports extended movement of the beholder's attention from part to part (Plate 12a). When the parts are fused and subordinated to a single emphatic focus, his attention is enabled to encompass the total material simultaneously, and while there is considerable invitation for the attention to move about along major axes, into spatial recessions, and over patterns of illumination and color, there is little possibility of its resting at any point (Plates 7b, 41). The choice between compositions supporting successive or simultaneous attention is therefore not a matter of absolute superiority of one over the other, but of their respective values for particular types of personality.

The former quality suggests the process of logical, scientific investigation in which a problem is resolved into component elements, each of which is given equal separate attention. This capacity for delaying concentration on a final solution while the component elements are investigated, expresses the self-confidence of human intelligence respecting its ability to solve the problem in due course; and also implies freedom from fear of mysterious supernatural opposition against which vigilance must never be relaxed.

Fusion of material in a work of art corresponds to the actual complexity of nature and of human experience, which is accepted in the sensational view as not being susceptible of profitable, significant, or interesting penetration by intelligent analysis. Analytical description of a phenomenon does not attempt to convey the actuality of experience but rather modifies it to the processes of human deliberation, whereas the sensational complexity of naturally fused experience must be grasped by unreflecting intuition.

In short, mechanical articulation of forms, in composition based on separate or discrete handling of detail, supports successive attention to uniformly emphatic and distinct parts, which provides an extended, leisurely experience. Fusion and interdependence of parts in the later, organic type of articulation, invites simultaneous attention made possible by various devices for contrasting emphasis and subordination of component parts, and constituting an experience of greater tension and excitement, which, however, cannot be long sustained. Roughly, among the pleasures of an amusement park, they might be said to correspond respectively to the cumulative satisfaction of the shooting gallery and the concentrated thrill of the roller coaster.

## CLEARNESS AND OBSCURITY

Although a loose reverence is generally accorded the cliché, "Truth is beauty and beauty, truth," it has been an accepted aim in art only for a comparatively brief period of Western civilization, during an early stage of Greek culture. How can it be applied to the two paintings of the *Pietà* shown in Plate 2? Furthermore the statement is relatively meaningless as a creative *program* since it ignores the basic alternative between two *kinds* of truth: one the penetrating generalization serviceable in the manipulation of environment; the other the naturalistic or subjective paraphrase of experience, intended to be evocative or entertaining. These are conveyed in the arts respectively by analytical and sensational style. The technical devices cited up to this point, as well as others, may be used by the artist either to clarify the structure of his composition and its references to objective reality or to contradict structural logic and call attention predominantly to the mysterious and unusual in the objective world. The term "objective" is used here to indicate the human experience *referred to* in a work of art as distinct from the aesthetic experience intrinsic in the work itself; for example, what is actually a circular area in a painting, of red-yellow hue modified with light and dark shading, refers *objectively* to a spherical form known in human experience as an orange.

In respect to the structure of a composition in the plastic arts, opposite tendencies to clarify or obscure may best be illustrated by architecture. In analytical styles of the past, frankness regarding means of construction has led to emphasizing joints in the stonework as an element in design; lower stories have been of heavier, simplified design (fewer and smaller windows, for example), with more elaborate or refined decoration reserved for upper areas; nonstructural decoration, like sculptural embellishment in Greek pediments and the metopes of the Doric order (Plate 9a), is confined to enclosed areas clearly relieved of any supporting function; and in general the design of the exterior clearly presents the supporting functions it performs and the articulation of interior spaces. In later periods a sensational emphasis appears as in other arts, which delights in devices seeming to deny structural logic and obscure functional reference. Support, for example, may be performed by spiral columns or by carved human figures suggesting a high degree of instability, or by slenderized and flowing curvilinear members like the quasi-naturalistic motifs of Rococo style (Plate 9b). Introduction of the giant order in the high Renaissance and Baroque periods obscures the existence of separate stories in a building, or where it actually does correspond to a large interior space, indicates the tendency toward emphasis and subordination shown in the previous section to characterize the sensational category of style. In sculpture a figure like Giovanni da Bologna's *Mercury* (Plate 14b) is of course similarly in conflict with the structural implications of the sculptural medium, both in the instability of its balance and the reference to motion.

The tendency of certain periods to reject clarity of exposition appears also in the way the objective world may be interpreted in the representational arts of painting and sculpture, even though the images may be *optically* convincing. For objective reference in sensational expression is essentially particularized, accidental, and momentary in its visual effect; and may also favor bizarre, quaint, or mysterious twists in treatment and selection of the subject. There is something of the "man bites dog" interest, or an attitude similar to the primitive view that only the unusual is important. Modern thought widely accepts the practical importance of basic generalities; but in art today they are apt to be considered boring or negligible. When broad and basic references are indicated for some monumental form of expression, it is generally felt either that they must be concealed in a pattern of immediate or topical reportage, especially in literature; or that any actuality must be eliminated by vaguely idealistic symbolism, as in most architectural sculpture. Mysterious, hilarious, or even revolting departures from the usual or expected are much more prevalent interests of the contemporary novel or drama (among those who currently follow those fields) than presentations of important human aims and accomplishments.

Optical treatment in the plastic arts not only directs attention away from primary qualities of an object's form, concealing outlines, upsetting structural logic and submerging detail, but it also complicates the presentation of color. True local color appears only in a few areas of halftone (neither highlight nor shadow) when illumination is emphasized in a painting. Other values are gained, to be sure, in the seventeenth century by dramatic chiaroscuro employing neutral pigments to create shadow, and in the range and luminosity of the full palette of later Impressionism. A literal statement regarding local color, however, is essentially incompatible with an emphasis on illumination, and the artist's choice signifies an expressive attitude consonant with the general aims of one or the other of the polar categories of style.

Another difference in relative clarity that may appear between analytical and sensational works, especially in the medium of painting, is the quantity of effort that has gone into their creation. The carefully drawn and detailed forms presented in early styles exhibit clearly the patient effort that has formed each part. In later styles so much of the effect depends on suggestion, on subtle or sweeping tonality, on manual skill refined to a virtuosity that prizes the appearance of effortlessness, that a quantitative estimate of the human exercise involved in the creation of a particular work of art can hardly be made simply by examination of the work itself. This effortless appearance is not an automatic result of increase in skill from generation to generation, but a deliberate concealment, in which the artist may actually discard any number of rapidly executed works in a medium like water color, preserving only those that "come off," so that the effort is not even physically present in the work selected for release. A great deal of preliminary effort is concealed by scraping and repainting certain areas in an oil painting until a desirable effect is obtained; glazing over a preliminary underpainting with sweeping tones to "pull the composition together" may also submerge or eliminate a considerable amount of detail; and such concealment is a primary aim of developing virtuosity of execution by means of elaborate and lengthy exercises of professional training in late styles of art.

To balance the precept relating truth and beauty, there is not only the objective of "the art that conceals art," but also art that conceals many other aspects of experience. They are concealed for the benefit of certain types of society or individual because they are deemed offensive, boring or expendable in the pursuit of more pleasant or intriguing qualities. When he is primarily concerned with the intrinsic experience of the work itself, the artist may choose to convey only those aspects that are sensuously exciting or ingratiating, regardless of their relative importance in the exposition of objective, plastic forms. When his interest is predominantly to reflect his environment, like that of French "boulevard realists" of the late nineteenth century (Plate 7a), he may nevertheless be more concerned with those highly personal or specific aspects which are informative only in the most fragmentary or oblique sense, rather than with hammering out basic, practical realities. An extreme comparison might be made between a Currier and Ives print on railroading and the painting called *Rain, Steam and Speed,* by the great British colorist J. M. W. Turner, now in the National Gallery in London. (Plate 10a and b.) Even in various night scenes, where car windows and headlights gleam in contrast with the surrounding darkness, no details of construction or activity are slighted in the prints, whereas in Turner's painting the train is hardly indentifiable as such, no structural details whatever are discernible, and the general effect is much closer to that of a burst of colorful light occurring in mid-air, than to any practical, mechanical activity.

## RHYTHM AND FLOW

One of the most confused areas in the analysis of style in the plastic mediums is that of "movement." The term of course refers to sensations of movement created by the aesthetic material of the work rather than by any reference to natural activity, which might be distinguished as "motion." The latter comes in for a certain amount of discussion, to be sure, relative to the ability of artists of any given period to represent such gestures as are seen in human athletics or the running gaits of animals. The erroneous "flying gallop" for example, was employed late into the nineteenth century, until instantaneous photography was able to expose the difference between the gallop of the horse and running gaits of other animals. This is essentially a technical rather than a stylistic concern.

Two fatal inaccuracies in the discussion of movement in art have been (1) to consider the polar categories of classical or analytical style and baroque or sensational style as respectively "static" and "dynamic"; and (2) the utterly thoughtless identification of the term "rhythm" with any type of compositional movement. Not all movement is rhythmical even in art, and to use the two terms interchangeably is to waste an important basis for distinction between analytical and sensational form. Both confusions may be eliminated by accurate distinction of the qualities of compositional movement, which is actually movement of the beholder's attention throughout the work induced by aesthetic elements rather than any reference to physical motion that might be suggested by the subject matter.

The "static-dynamic" dichotomy is useless because all works of art of any complexity or composition whatsoever involve some movement. Actually the painters of the Florentine proto-Renaissance, with their "Salome" figures and the studies of motion by the Naturalists, display as much *interest* in movement as those of the Baroque. The difference is simply that the aesthetic approach of the later period lends itself better to the interpretation of motion. There is more sense of movement from part to part in a Baroque portrait, like Bernini's Louis XIV, than in a Uccello battle piece (Plate 11a and b); and this is equally true of the movement in an apparently quiet Dutch seventeenth-century interior, though not as obviously (Plate 39a). The most serviceable polarity that can be identified respecting aesthetic movement or movement of composition is between the *rhythmic* relation of separate, static units, as against the continuous *flow* of movement through intimately fused parts.

The generalized, clarifying treatment of form in analytical styles tends to eliminate accidental aspects of objects revealed in motion, and to establish a sense of enduring sculpturesque bulk that might be called static. However, in addition to the equivalence of emphasis on objects throughout an analytical composition, there is also a remarkably close equivalence of interval between them, which sets up a clear rhythmic relationship. Attention rests and jumps in a measured movement that might be compared to a classical colonnade or musical accent. Even the spatial background in such a composition is laid out with major structural divisions and axes at rhythmic intervals. This is quite clear in Carpaccio's *Dream of St. Ursula,* as well as the other paintings in this series (Plate 12a), and forms an important part of the aesthetic distinction of still-life paintings by Chardin. In sensational styles the fusion of one figure with another, destruction of limiting contours, development of evanescent surface illumination, all destroy the sense of anchored weight, and facilitate a dancing flow of attention hither and yon. Centrifugal radiation of the composition from a highly emphasized focus assures a constant flow of attention outward and back.

One of the alternatives, then, which an artist may choose, contributing to the total stylistic effect either of an analytical or sensational approach to the creative process, is between *rhythm* and *flow* in the movement of the composition. Another alternative in the quality of movement is also distinguishable, namely, whether or not the forces in the composition seem to be balanced by equal distribution or by various sorts of tension between unequal parts.

## BALANCE AND TENSION

A feeling of greater or less movement in composition may be set up by the relative balance or imbalance of its masses. When the major compositional volumes are relatively equivalent the resulting sense of balance yields an expression of calmly coordinated forces. When they are unequal they must be held together in composition by implied tensions which create a sense of strain and excitement. Thus in a composition like Degas' *At the Races* (Plate 7b), the artist has not discarded the notion of balance in putting the carriage on one side of the picture instead of centering it. Its mass is balanced on the "yardarm" principle with the small figures in the background, which gain leverage by their distance from the center of the composition, as from a fulcrum. In order to realize this type of balance, the beholder must keep the several factors constantly in mind, which creates a tension and interdependence in the design characteristic of sensational style.

Another form of tension in art appears in the tendency of certain styles to animate the entire composition with a pervasive activity that may appear highly arbitrary in terms of the subjects represented and tends to confer a decidedly crowded feeling on the spatial arrangement. Early medieval art, as in Hiberno-Saxon manuscript illumination (Plate 20), frequently prolongs terminal features and involves them in elaborate convolutions. Another device for heightening movement is fluttering the drapery and blowing in bits of cloud so that no area is permitted to subside into a relieving calm (Plate 35c). A similar but less arbitrary crowding of the composition is characteristic of Baroque style. In a manner to be discussed more fully later, considerable anxiety is expressed in both these instances, that of the earlier primitive expression being more cosmic, naïve and frank; that of the later sophisticated style more socially oriented, and disguising its tensions in formal patterns expressing a certain limited self-assurance.

The alternatives of balance and tension are also embodied in the proportioning of masses and spaces. Representational art may limit or exaggerate the difference between the length and breadth of figures for a variety of purposes. Generally, added height in human figures represents grace, elegance and nobility; breadth confers ridicule or vulgarity. Greek art within a century changed the canonical proportion of the human body from seven to eight heads, but a comparison of extremes from African Negro sculpture to some Byzantine and Romanesque examples of elongation shows a range of about four to twelve or more (Plate 13). Most of this of course is determined by expressive requirements of the style rather than by any attempt to confer a particular human quality on the figures. In architecture, proportion is one of the most important elements of the expressive vocabulary.

A great deal of mystification asises from claims of "perfection" for the proportion of the "Golden Section." This is a ratio in which the smaller quantity is to the larger as the larger is to their sum, or a:b::b: a + b. It expresses maximum relaxation, for it is necessarily less than two to one. Thus it would be fine for a high Renaissance door, window or the spacing of fenestration and colonnades in this style; but is meaningless for the description of a column or human figure, and completely anathematizes the tension and refinement that is the essence of Gothic architecture, as well as many other highly admired forms and styles throughout the history of art.

Proportion is related to movement in art by way of the empathy with which the aesthetic content of all works of art must be transcribed into human sensory experience. Styles have uniformly tended to develop from balanced proportion toward tension. The change from a familiar, canonical Doric colomn seven lower diameters in height to one of nine, or to an Ionic column of eleven or more, suggests a *stretching* of the heavier shape, implying a force that remains stored in the elongated shape and becomes an element of tension in the composition. When a shape assumes the extreme proportions of a Gothic column rib or an interlaced animal from an early medieval manuscript, it loses virtually all sense of bulk and conveys merely a sense of movement. Any major axis, especially in architecture, has this linear, directional implication, and the force of the axial movement increases as the area or volume attenuates.

Perhaps the most pervasive sense of tension is set up by the tendency toward fusion or interdependence of all the elements of composition in a sensational style. The self-contained units of works in analytical styles are sufficiently independent, as has been indicated, to receive the beholder's complete and leisurely attention as it moves successively from part to part. In sensational works, however, attention is constantly led or pulled from one interdependent part to another. This restlessness may be swaggering or graceful in an Italian Baroque mural, cramped and uneasy in a Romanesque tympanum, but both embody a sense of tension that is absent even from as emotional a work as Mantegna's *Crucifixion* or *Christ on the Mount of Olives,* as gay a work as Botticelli's *Primavera,* or as active a one as a battle piece by Uccello.

So it is in personal conduct. There are some who cannot function without working themselves into a Napoleonically sleepless furor, which eventually or periodically destroys them. Others function in a measured rhythm of full but calm application that must give way to compensating periods of relaxed recreation and a night's sleep.

SUMMARY: TABLE OF THE POLAR CATEGORIES

The foregoing description of opposite qualities of form in the plastic arts may be summarized and correlated in a tabular arrangement. This table should be read as a series of simple, declarative sentences by repeating the caption of each column before the particular terms in a horizontal sequence, thus: "In respect to substantiation or description, analytical form is tactile, using line; sensational form is optic, using tone," and so on.

| In respect to: | Analytical Form is: | Sensational Form is: |
|---|---|---|
| Substantiation or description | Tactile (using line) | Optic (using tone) |
| Space | Planimetric | Recessional |
| Composition | Closed or enframed | Open or focused and radiating |
| Articulation | Mechanical, with separate or discrete parts supporting successive attention | Organic, with fused or interdependent parts inducing simultaneous attention |
| Structure and exposition | Clarified | Obscure |
| Movement | Rhythmic and balanced | Flowing and intensified |

A structure and vocabulary is thus established whereby the differences in appearance between one work of art and another that are indicated by the term "style" may be described and related without recourse to the subjective, historical and otherwise imprecise terminology that has abounded so confusingly throughout the criticism of the arts. The reader must make a special effort to realize that the terms "analysis and sensation, analytical and sensational," will be used hereafter in these pages only in the precise and limited sense indicated.

*Style in art might be defined as those aspects of form that are correlated to produce a socially desirable expression consciously or unconsciously intended by the artist.* It has already been noted that the tendency of the characteristics to cohere interdependently in two opposite categories (linear description serves clarity of articulation, clarity of articulation serves rhythmic movement, and so on) suggests a common expressive motivation. This common motivation which arises from the cultural homogeneity of the period or group for which the art is produced, is basic throughout the plastic arts and has clear parallels in the performing arts. Consequently such attempts as have frequently been made to ascribe characteristics of style to fortuitous technological factors which would affect only one medium must be discarded.

A flagrant example of what might be called the technological fallacy was the general attribution a few decades ago of the linear quality in fifteenth-century Florentine work, and thence the Italian Renaissance generally, to the prevalence of the fresco medium for mural decoration. The suggestion was that the transference of the cartoon to the wall by a tracing of the outline tended to induce a concern with contours. Such an explanation does not encompass the fact that a similar linear quality characterizes fifteenth-century art in Flanders where mural painting was not practiced to any extent in fresco or any other medium; and that as Italian culture became more interested in fused and optic style, new mediums were readily introduced in Italy for mural decoration. The fact that the linear quality of fifteenth- and sixteenth-century style is associated with other elements of similarly analytical character points clearly to a motivation outside the requirements or limitations of medium. The technique of fresco painting, for example, could not by any stretch of the imagination be made to account for planimetric space. As a matter of fact, stylistic requirements are generally the basis for changes in technical practice, frequently inspiring the invention of completely new mediums. This is most notable perhaps in the development of print making from the beginning of the Reformation when a widespread attempt to influence popular culture first began.

The comparatively linear and rigid mediums of wood block and engraving were invented and carried to their highest form (in the work of Albrecht Dürer) within a single century. When tonality and fusion requiring a fluid, speedy execution became the general character of style in the plastic arts, etching was promptly invented and again carried almost immediately to its highest development by Rembrandt. Lithography was invented in the nineteenth century for increased production to satisfy a new surge in the spread of cultural interest engendered by the growth of political democracy and popular education in the Industrial Revolution, and also to relieve the artist of technical concerns in an age that chose to differentiate drastically between the material and spiritual, bestowing a kind of contempt on the mechanics of artistic creation. Clearly, any influence between expression and technique or medium runs from the former to the latter and not in the opposite direction.

*Application to Sculpture.* Although most painters think of themselves as quite different from sculptors, and most architects think of themselves as vastly different from both, there are a number of sculptors today whose careers started with the study of painting; and in the Renaissance many painters and sculptors were also architects, Raphael, Michelangelo and Bernini being among the leaders in this type of versatility. These three mediums, sometimes called the spatial as well as the plastic arts, are aesthetically homogeneous in their common function of employing mass and space to create or embellish human environment. The other great family of the arts, of course, is the group of the performing arts—music, dance and drama—or the arts of time, whose function is to create or embellish human occasions. Some indication has already been made of the applicability of the terminology here presented throughout the plastic or spatial arts, but the chief emphasis has been on painting. The matter of stylistic motivation may be clarified, however, by a brief examination of the possibilities of using the polar categories for the analysis of style in sculpture and architecture.

How can sculpture be analyzed in relation to the elements of line and tone, which seem to be technical means employed only in painting? Aesthetically, of course, line in painting is an analytical, tactile device and tone is its sensational counterpart conveying a basically optic impression. Likewise the forms of sculpture may be clarified by emphasizing the continuity of surface in the major volumes to produce a predominantly tactile effect, conferring an analytical quality on the work. However, it is also possible to elaborate the surface with greater attention to details, emphasizing contrasts of light and shadow which sensuously enrich the general effect, although they may tend to sacrifice some realization of the basic masses. Hellenistic work such as the *Laocoön* and the Great Altar at Pergamon (Plate 4b), Michelangelo's *Slaves* (Plate 14a), and occasional passages in his later work, as well as most of the work of Rodin (who is sometimes called a "romantic impressionist," a term more commonly employed in relation to painting), display this optic treatment of sculpture in association with other sensational qualities. A common device in this type of sculpture is the tendency to leave parts of carvings rough or "unfinished," or to allow separate lumps of clay to remain evident and incompletely smoothed out in figures for bronze casting, to preserve optically exciting modulations of surface tones and textures.

Softening of detail and contours between forms in contact is also used for this purpose.

*Contrapposto,* or turning the parts of a figure in different directions, is an attempt to increase the sense of spatial volume and circulation in free-standing sculpture, which is clearly a *recessional* treatment of space although no great distance is involved. A similar aspect of recessional composition of relief sculpture was described above in reference to the motion of figures in the Great Altar of Pergamon toward and away from the relief plane, which is thus completely demolished as a palpable aesthetic element. Bernini's niche tombs, like that of Pope Alexander VII (Plate 15), set up a recessional relation between the major figure, the enframement of the niche, and the symbolic minor figures, which are distributed in front of and behind both the pedestal and frame. The manner in which the figures break out of the enframing niche is also clearly an example of the *open form* of composition in sculpture.

Closed and open form in painting is characterized by the relation of the masses and space of the composition to the frame and the picture plane, which do not exist for sculpture in the round except insofar as they may be provided by elements of an architectural setting. However, certain pieces of sculpture are seen to be composed, as Michelangelo said, "so that if they were rolled downhill, no parts would break off." Such a figure appears to be enclosed in an invisible capsule which it touches at a number of points but exceeds at none, and this might be considered comparable to the picture plane in painting. Some reality exists for this capsule or envelope when it is thought of as the original surface of the block from which the figure was made (if a carving), or as a volume of space defined by extending the outer edge of the base vertically to the top of the figure's head. In this sense also, the pedestal of a piece of sculpture in the round, with its horizontal moldings emphasizing the area of the column, implies a sort of frame.

None of these strictures, which obviously pertain to *closed form* in sculpture, have any meaning relative to *open* compositions like Giovanni da Bologna's *Mercury* (Plate 14b), Bernini's *Ecstasy of Santa Theresa,* or the Hellenistic *Nike of Samothrace* (Plate 16b), all of which radiate as from a central focus, and bevel off gradually into the circumambient. A maximum sense of spatial continuity with the surrounding environment is thus maintained. The *Nike of Samothrace,* moreover, which represents the Goddess of Victory alighting on the deck of a ship, is mounted on a pedestal built in the form of the copper-beaked prow of a

Greek naval vessel and was placed at one end of a pool of water, establishing a meaningful continuum with environment somewhat similar to the "grotto" sculptures of the Baroque, or Tiepolo's murals in the Palazzo Labia, described above (Plate 6).

Extreme geometrical simplification and mechanical separation of parts is noted in African Negro sculpture (Plate 12b), Egyptian sculpture (Plate 30a), and archaic Greek (Plate 22). Considerable clarity of anatomical detail is apparent even in a fifth-century B.C. Greek work like the *Spearbearer* of Polykleitos (Plate 16a), as particularly in the sharply defined groin line and pectoral muscles. In the following century, however, surface anatomy was considerably softened, as in the work of Praxiteles, and although much anatomical detail appears in Hellenistic sculpture, as of the Pergamene school for example, it does not have the patterned clarity of early Greek work, but rather a particularized and exhaustive quality following the complexity of natural, organic articulation, and tending to produce optic sensations of light and shade by means of very deep modeling of the surface.

Structural contradiction in sculpture has already been pointed out in the toe-balanced figure of Bologna's *Mercury* (Plate 14b). Sculptural virtuosity in later periods also produces surprising plastic contradictions in the imitation of insubstantial materials like hair, lace, and other fabrics. Extreme examples may be found among the portraits of the Italian Baroque sculptor Bernini (Plate 11b), and in the general Baroque tendency to convey clouds, foliage and water as well as close imitations of clothing in stone or bronze. In Bernini's famous *Chair of St. Peter*, forming the main altarpiece of St. Peter's Church in the Vatican, the principal object occupies a focal point considerably above the ground level, held up by human hands, a host of angels floats among still higher clouds, and even rays of light are represented by sculptured bronze!

Respecting movement, the limited compositional possibilities of sculpture in the round makes the application of the polarity of *rhythm* and *flow* less obvious except in respect to the handling of detail such as clothing or anatomy. However, it may be significant for the interpretation of mid-twentieth-century style, that with the invention of the "mobile," sculpture becomes the only plastic medium that attempts to embody *actual* movement in design (except for the use of decorative water fountains in architecture, definitely a late, sensational innovation also).

*Application to Architecture.* Even more striking than the pertinence of this terminology, developed primarily for painting, to sculpture, a medium using actual mass and space instead of two-dimensional illusions, is the application of precisely the same terminology of stylistic analysis to the nonrepresentational forms in architecture. Since the edge of a piece of building material must be precise regardless of style, some confusion may arise in differentiating *line* and *tone*. However, it is clear that the salient cornices, moldings and window embrasures of late Renaissance and Baroque buildings add a pattern of light and shadow to the exterior that is not felt in the less prominently relieved façades of fifteenth- and sixteenth-century buildings. A contrast of the finely carved detail of fifth-century B.C. capitals and entablatures in Greece with the more prolific detail of Hellenistic and Roman buildings reveals a clear interest in realizing the tactile reality of each component in the earlier work; whereas the apparently careless, mass production of moldings and capitals on the colossal Roman structures contributes rather a generalized optic elaboration of a total area through contrast of light and dark, with little independent reality in the particular motif. In a finely carved Greek cornice, the "egg" in an egg-and-dart molding immediately suggests a delightful fullness in the hollow of one's palm; the "darts" cause the finger tips to tingle with anticipation of running back and forth along their fine, gently curved edges. The acanthus leaves on a Greek Corinthian capital stand out crisply, and the elaborate pattern of their outlines remains clear as it winds tortuously around the separate lobes; but in a Roman Corinthian capital, the complex pattern is more likely to be indicated merely with a few lines and "eyes" made by the drill to suggest simply the optic effect of the leafy cone rather than to produce a full tactile realization of the elaborately convoluted surfaces.

The tendency to elongate the nave of the basilica type of church in Western Europe during the Middle Ages (Plate 17a and b), as against the continued popularity of the Greek cross plan (Plate 17c), octagonal and other "central" plans in the eastern Mediterranean areas, obviously affords an opportunity for emphasis of recessional vistas on the interior. The repeated revisions of the plans for St. Peter's in Rome by several generations of architects is especially interesting in this connection. A central plan was envisaged from the beginning, up through the design of Michelangelo, who actually constructed the crossing as far as the base of the dome (carried out later in accordance with his design), as an equal-armed "Greek cross." It was not until the Baroque period that the western arm was elongated, imparting to the building the imbalance and recessional space of the sensational category.

Recessional accent is created further in St. Peter's by Bernini's colonnaded approach on the exterior (which is likewise a device for "opening" the composition). The straight portions of the colonnade as they approach the façade are not at right angles to it, so that the sense of perspective is heightened. Contemporary sketches also indicate the intention of partly closing the present wide space in the opposite end of the oval, leaving entrances off center at either side to prevent approach to the building on axis, thus presenting the façade with its piazza always in angular perspective.

The elaborated doorways of Baroque churches, like the columned portals of Gothic and some other medieval churches, set up a recession of forms which not only give depth to the façade itself, but suggest movement from the exterior to the interior. The variation in shapes and sizes of the successive rooms in late Roman monumental architecture, notably the baths (Plate 33a), again suggests an interest in the recessional vista, as the spectator peers from one large space through a somewhat constricted passage, vestibule, or anteroom into another more open section.

Elimination of the atrium, or enclosed forecourt, from the medieval basilica in favor of the open square suggesting greater continuity with its surroundings, may have been as much a practical as a stylistic change. The devout became less distinct from the rest of the community; the need for occasional defense against predatory violence subsided. However, the gradual development of the exterior of the medieval basilica to the sculptural glory of the high Gothic cathedral façade (Plate 18b) may be interpreted as a tendency toward open, radiating composition, as well as a doctrinaire change in the position of the Church, from a distinct, as it were extraterritorial, display of heaven on earth, to an integrated cultural focus of the community.

The finials, crocketing, and flying buttresses, furthermore, bevel the mass of the building gradually into surrounding space, as do the wings of the *Nike of Samothrace* (Plate 16b), or the outstretched arms of the familiar *Mercury* (Plate 14b). The tendency to mount sculptured figures against the sky above columns on a Baroque façade has a similar beveling or radiating effect.

Another device for weakening the outer limits of the design in Baroque architecture is to extend the *actual forms of the building* beyond the *apparent limits of the design*. This is the significance, for example, of adding an unemphatic attic story above the main cornice or pediment, and of not permitting a colonnade to extend the full length of the façade it decorates. An interesting transition is the Palladian design, for church façades, of interpenetrating pedimented colonnades, characteristic of the Venetian high Renaissance (Plate 18a).

Organic fusion of parts is most evident in the foliate, curvilinear decoration of the Rococo style (Plate 9b). Emphasis on central units to which other parts are subordinated, as in Baroque architecture, tends to create a fusion of the total pattern. The plan of a Romanesque basilica generally shows considerable salience of separate transepts and radiating chapels, conferring a general appearance of prismatic subdivision on the east end (Plate 17a). Though there is no reduction in the structural or decorative complexity of a Gothic cathedral, the distinct parts are gradually merged into an organic whole, with transepts shortened and chapels ranged in continuous sequence (Plate 17b).

Later styles characteristically employ considerable ingenuity in obscuring structural requirements. Most notable, perhaps, are the addition of structurally useless lierne ribs in Gothic vaulting of the Flamboyant period, and the development of fan vaulting (Plate 19a), which abandoned not only the structural significance of the rib as a means of support, but also the clear division into bays characteristic of the high Gothic four-part rib vault. Structural realities of architectural design are likewise obscured in later periods by twisted columns, supports carved in the shape of human or animal figures, and other devices for weakening the appearance of solidity in supporting members (Plate 9b).

Adherence to the vocabulary of the classical orders enforces a certain amount of rhythmic repetition in a Baroque design, but everything possible is done to complicate the measure so that it may lead up to a climactic emphasis on a central unit instead of distributing uniform stress throughout a series. Thus, although the main design of a Baroque church façade might be an equal series of Corinthian columns, other columns or pilasters are introduced about the doorway, and each column may be backed up with single or double pilasters. Some columns are emphasized by the coincidence of other members or pieces of sculpture in the upper ranges, so that the rhythmic character of the basic colonnade is highly complicated or virtually lost.

The same tendencies toward attenuation of proportion, characteristic of late periods in sculpture, follow similarly in architecture. The canonical proportion of columns in the Greek orders became more slender almost from decade to decade during the period of their most intense development, as did the proportions of Gothic ribs, the plan of the bay, height and length of the nave, and other ratios in the Gothic cathedral. The balanced semicircle of the arch in Romanesque architecture gave way to the high, stilted, and pointed Gothic arch. The round arch of the Renaissance, however, was replaced by the flattened oval arches of the Baroque, and the oval was frequently used at that time in plan also.

"Scale" is another important aspect of proportion in the plastic arts, especially architecture. The term refers not to the ratio of related dimensions within the work itself, but to the relation of its general dimensions to the size of objects in its environment, primarily the human figure. In the early Renaissance, for example, there was no particular stress on size, and a large building would be designed as a series of distinct parts or courses, "scaled down" to some commensurability with human size. In Baroque architecture, however, the tendency is to fuse the entire design into the maximum scale, largely by use of the giant order (that is, columns running the full height of the façade regardless of any horizontal subdivision of the interior space). The bases of the columns in St. Peter's are about as tall as a person, and the only way he can relate himself to forms of such magnitude is as a negligible quantity (Plate 19b).

*Indications of a Common Motivation.* This rapid survey of the application of the polar categories of style to sculpture and architecture is, of course, far from complete. It is intended in part to indicate the serviceability of the polar categories for the analysis of style throughout the plastic arts; but beyond that, to demonstrate the fact that all mediums employing masses and spaces for the creation and embellishment of environment follow a common pattern of design. Examples from one medium may thus be used to clarify the aesthetic intention in another; but more important is the incontestable indication that the motivation for such design cannot come from intrinsic aesthetic or material considerations of the mediums themselves. If the latter were true, no such commonality would develop, for the requirements of painting on wood, paper, or canvas must of necessity be vastly different from the considerations of modeling or carving natural forms, and from structure and function in the enclosure of space for public or private use; hence no such striking parallels as have been indicated could arise.

The polar categories here described quite accurately embrace the plastic arts, but a similar analysis might be made of style in the performing arts, especially music. Curt Sachs has done a great deal along these lines in his *Commonwealth of Art.* Any stylistic analysis of music in terms of the polar categories and the motivations here suggested, however, must take into account the fact that the abstract instrumental performances developed during the past few centuries independent of verbal text are in some ways entirely sensational. Bach and Mozart are definitely more "linear," in the contrapuntal structure of their works, than Debussy or Wagner. But before them, and indeed continuing in the church music and operas of Bach and Mozart, music was an ancillary, though often substantial, element of the performing or dramatic arts.

The evolution of the symphony and succeeding instrumental forms is far from being the entire history of music. The divorcement of musical instrumentation from some form of verbal expression is in itself a kind of major transition toward sensation. In similar fashion, all styles of painting in Western Europe after the early fifteenth century are sensational in respect to the illusion of space, though the illusion itself may be achieved either analytically or sensationally by the use of plane or recession.

Thus the question, "How does Bach's linear type of music arise in a Baroque period of the plastic arts, if style is socially motivated?" must be answered by pointing out that the development of an independent role for instrumental music is itself a sensational development appropriate to Baroque society. Beyond that point, musical style grows increasingly *more* sensational, just as nineteenth-century impressionist painting is far more sensational in some respects than any painting of the seventeenth century. It is certainly more optic, and more fused—at least in material substance if not in design. Next to Monet, Rubens is tactile, clarified, and even somewhat planimetric (compare Plates 40b and 41).

Identity of aesthetic quality and evolutionary tendencies throughout such broad and complex areas must indicate a common motivation for those aspects of plastic creation that are called "style." Style is motivated by the role the work of art must play in expressing the cosmic and social philosophies of the societies for which it is produced. It remains to describe the general types of motivation engendering recourse to one or the other category of style, so that the expression of the forms may be reasonably and objectively interpreted. Incidentally, the discovery that certain qualities of form have expressive values for one culture which would be meaningless or distasteful for another should clear up a considerable amount of semantic garbage clinging to criticism of the arts in the form of irrelevant pontifical absolutes, from bygone eras, that have caused immeasurable confusion.

Whereas virtuosity stands for excellence in one context, its opposite "sound craftsmanship" will be extolled in another. "Static" is virtually a term of derogation in contemporary cultural criticism; yet in other fields calm, balance, and restraint are terms of strong positive connotation. Humanism is vastly admired today (under a variety of almost contradictory forms), yet many of the most acclaimed cultural expressions in literature and drama are highly individualistic, pessimistic, and derogatory of human motives and institutions. Little agreement can be found even on what most clearly presents "reality" in art. This is because the counterfeit of natural vision that is accomplished by optic realism in the representational arts has a certain obviousness which tends to overshadow other superiorities of tactile representation. Early, linear works seem "stiff" and "naïve" to many people, in contrast with the virtuosity and dynamic qualities of sensational style. Yet in architecture, critics from the neoclassic movement of the eighteenth century to the present have deplored some attractive qualities in the Baroque as a "decadence" from the more static quality of Renaissance work. Renaissance architects themselves anathematized the "barbarous" lack of logic and restraint in medieval architecture, giving it the name of "Gothic" to characterize its barbarity.

Clarification of critical value and terminology is needed, not to determine what is good and bad, but what any given quality is good *for*. Obviously analysis leading to conclusions of the former type is purely subjective, valid only in respect to limited, particular aims. Subsequent discussion of the motives for using one polar category of style or the other will not only serve to supply an objective means of determining the kind of value available to a sympathetic personality in any given style of art, but also will enable the critic to read back from the form of the work, the aims and attitudes of the sponsoring society.

# 3

# Meaning of the Polar Categories

BOTH OBJECTIVE OR ECONOMIC AND SUBJECTIVE OR PSYCHOANALYTIC AREAS of the social sciences in modern times see the development of human society and human personality as a process of struggle, of action and re-action, of opposites working upon one another to produce something new and different. Whereas history at one time seemed to present human society in a series of static formulations like stage sets in successive acts of a conventional drama, with change confined to meaningless moments of upheaval from which the audience may be spared in the theater by lowering the curtain, it is now recognized that periods of complete stasis or balance are rare and brief. Change goes on all the time, perhaps on a molecular level the direction of which may not become fully apparent until there is a quantitative shift in the relation between the interacting forces. Although cultural expression, too, evolves in a similarly gradual fashion, the process can be much more readable in the stylistic evolution of works of art if they are properly understood.

At one time the fall of the Roman Empire was described more or less as a cataclysmic conquest by "barbarian hordes." It has since been pointed out, however, that barbarians quite familiar and sympathetic with Latin culture functioned for generations as thoroughly integrated elements of Roman society. Justinian the Great was born a barbarian, but in the Ravenna mosaics he stands a Roman with his empress Theodora and their retinues, wearing Roman togas, posed under round arches; and on close examination the "unrealistic" Byzantine style in which they are represented shows clear vestiges of Roman illusionism (Plate 32b).

"Napoleon revolutionized European life," said the historians of yesterday. "Napoleon's regime codified the accomplishments of the bourgeois revolution," say the historians of today. The word "bourgeois," city dweller, indicates a force that had been growing since the thirteenth century with the rise of the "communes," as many of the new or reorganized towns were called. Resurgent Florence, Paris, and London already had ancient histories, which started when they were peripheral Roman settlements. If Methuselah had lived in one of them, would he have been able to recognize just when it ceased to be a provincial outpost and began its development into a national capital? Lorenzo de' Medici was not the first of his dynasty, yet he was not handed absolute power by virtue of birth like an Egyptian pharaoh, but had to build it arduously, ingeniously, and perilously. There were grand gestures like suppression of the Pazzi conspiracy, with the public spectacle of traitors swinging in the Piazza della Signoria; but there was also much day by day bargaining, threatening, and forming of alliances with groups and individuals in terms of their mutual interests.

Therefore it is not surprising that the influences formulating the basic character of expression in art throughout the history of human culture must be stated in terms of "struggle." Connotations of violence and emotional strain that have grown up around this word, however, must be discounted. Perhaps the idea is closer to "striving," but this word is less serviceable in some respects. In any case, a term implying dynamic tendencies is required to account for cultural change. Growth in society is only metaphorically like a plant whose stem and leaves put forth buds, that burgeon into flowers and become fruit and seed. Actually it is more clearly reflected in the removal of trees and rocks to make a clearing in the wilderness, in which a house is built by hewing and pounding these natural materials into serviceable shape.

*Style in art is the resultant and the expression of creative struggle in three general areas: the struggle of man with his natural environment, the artist's own struggle with his means of expression, and the struggle of man for the betterment and control of society.* The first imparts a general character to all art of a given broad locality, persisting almost timelessly side by side with other types of influence with which it combines in differing degrees. The other two areas of struggle affect the changes which take place in a given culture as its development progresses. The three will here be described respectively as the ethnic or geographical, the technological, and the socioeconomic influences on style. Theoretically all of these influences are always present, but at different times their respective force varies to such an extent that one or two may appear to be absent or insignificant. Technological influence is in many ways parallel with or corollary to the socioeconomic, but there are certain values in giving it separate consideration.

Past interpretations of style in the arts have been greatly concerned with tracing the provenience and modification of motifs. Little thought has been given, however, to the reasons behind such adoptions and adaptations. Fortuitous contacts and the personal concern of prominent individuals seemed sufficient, and the classic revival in the Renaissance, for example, has been explained as being due to Niccolo Pisano's interest in the Roman sarcophagi of the Campo Santo in his native Pisa. Certain aspects of pattern in European painting of the late nineteenth century are attributed to the interest in Japanese prints first brought to Western attention when they were stuffed around fragile articles for protection in shipping; as though anyone would bother to read the old newspapers used here in the same fashion, unless he were a certain kind of person.

Presented as mechanical, fortuitous linkages, this sort of thing is relatively meaningless except for establishing purely historical sequence, and can indeed be misleading. How was it that the Roman sarcophagi and other perfectly apparent vestiges of classical culture throughout Italy went unnoticed until the thirteenth century? What is the difference between Pisano's response to classical example and that of later artists— Botticelli, Raphael or Bernini—not to mention earlier ones (which of course there were), like the illuminators of manuscripts for the court of Charlemagne? Recourse to stylistic models in this way is actually the result, not the cause of stylistic influences.

The term "influence" here refers specifically to forces inducing the taste of the artist and the society for which he works to prefer one or the other of the poles of stylistic expression—analytical or sensational—

which have been described at some length as definitely reflecting characteristic human responses to environment. The significant pattern of influence is the dynamic relation between the form or style of an object, the human attitude that would confer such qualities on form, and the type of culturally significant experience that would produce such an attitude.

## THE ARTIST AND HIS NATURAL ENVIRONMENT—
### ETHNIC OR GEOGRAPHICAL MOTIVATION

The struggle with nature was the crucial factor in the earliest periods of human culture, up through the beginnings of recorded history. The less strenuous climate in the southern portions of Europe, the lands bordering the Mediterranean Sea, was more hospitable to the human race, control must have developed faster, and survival was won with less pressure and fear of catastrophe than in lands too far from the equator. Consequently it was there that the concept of an anthropocentric world first came into being, of a natural order ordained to serve the needs of the human race. This concept bears the reassuring corollary that the only "secret" of nature is an orderly pattern of cause and effect readily susceptible of control by the characteristically human capacity for logical analysis. Hence, a predominantly analytical tendency affects cultural expression throughout southern Europe.

Human culture was conversely affected by the more difficult climatic situation in the north. The growing season is much shorter in Germany than in Italy, for example, and therefore men in the north must work under much greater pressure to produce the year's sustenance; and also there must have been considerably more anxiety in the earliest stages as to whether each year's supply would last until the following harvest. The rigor of winters in the north necessitated substantial shelter, and personal catastrophe due to climatic factors was more prevalent.

Such conditions reduced man's concept of his status to that of a hard-pressed adversary of his natural environment. Much greater power than his own logical intelligence seemed necessary to combat the antagonistic will he saw behind events that cruelly victimized him. Despite the capacity for survival he experienced as a group, he felt belittled, harried, anxious.

Furthermore, since it was only possible for mankind to develop initially under the most favorable conditions, in the great semitropical river valleys or "hothouse" situations, those who came later to inhabit other localities by virtue of the unique adaptability of the human race, must have given up a more favorable for a less favorable abode. Since it is inconceivable that this would be done voluntarily, there is ground for the belief that an element of force may have been involved. In other words, the man of the north may not only have felt himself the victim of natural forces, but he may have come there with a sense of exclusion and privation already inflicted upon him by a somehow more favored order of men.

These difficult conditions of life engendered the awe, humility, and confusion which deferred, in the culture of the north, the attempting of any logical penetration or mastery of natural processes. Groping intuition and mystical revelation were the only alternatives, resulting in sensational interpretations of form for cultural expression. Being attempts to appease or exorcise antagonistic cosmic forces, they were necessarily produced under great emotional tension regarding the ends to be achieved and the adequacy of the effort. Clear examples of this quality as it has persisted into recent times is seen in the nervous activity of early medieval manuscript styles in the north (Plate 20) and the exhaustive repetition of surface detail in fifteenth-century Flemish painting (Plate 21a and 8a).

Subsequently, of course, as agricultural and other techniques, along with related elaboration of the social structure, gradually overcame the major uncertainties in the struggle with nature, other factors arose to determine the character of form in cultural expression. But this primitive ethnic or geoclimatic factor had such profound influence originally that it has persisted, albeit with constantly diminishing force, practically to the present. Latter-day criticism has consistently recognized the tendency of northern European styles toward a complexity or exuberance which may accurately be defined by reference to the sensational or Baroque group of characteristics as opposed to the analytical or classic. Insufficient attention has been given, however, to the identification of this tendency with human reaction to northern environment, and to the human basis for the corresponding tendency of analytical characteristics to appear in the art of southern European or Mediterranean cultures. The mere observation of local characteristics may lead to certain confusions, as when they are not adequately distinguished from evolutionary influences, or in attempts to ascribe them to some quasi-biological form of racial inheritance.

*Mediterranean Expression.* The general character of the art of ancient Greece, as an example of early southern style, was certainly analytical. Its objective was the expression of an "ideal" beauty of the human figure, arrived at by conscious development of a canon of proportion among clearly articulated and generalized parts of the body. Objects represented in sculpture or painting were composed spatially in strict accord with the surface to which they were attached or related, and practically no representations of deep space were attempted until the rise of Levantine Hellenism. There is no merging of forms in composition, and even where overlapping appears, the full exposition of each figure is clearly suggested. Rhythmic continuity is used for compositional coherence, and overshadowing stress on principal figures is avoided, although unemphatic central placing is used to distinguish them in simple, bisymmetrical arrangements, such as a sculptured pediment.

This simplicity and clarity of structure corresponds to the conceptual character of Greek religion, which envisioned a clear distribution of legislative and judicial powers or jurisdictions among a number of manlike gods related to one another much in the manner of a large human family. Prayers in one direction, fiats in the other, proceeded in direct logical fashion. A mere man or group of men could offend or propitiate the gods and be meted a direct, calculable return for value received, much as in a modern political machine. There was no mystery about why the Trojans lost the war. Pallas Athena brought it about quite simply for reasons that were clear and sufficient to herself, in terms of personal pique readily understandable by any human. It was not primarily the mysterious caprice of impenetrable natural forces that drove Aeneas about the Mediterranean for many years, but the smoldering resentment of Juno against the Trojans, who had offended within her official jurisdiction when they broke the connubial union of Helen and Menelaus, as Virgil is careful to recall in considerable detail at the opening of his *Aeneid.*

*Northern Expression.* In the religions of the north, however, there is neither clear distribution of powers among the gods, nor an obvious pattern of its application. The gods, indeed, are not even all-powerful, for there are mysterious giants with infinitely superior force in certain spheres, and a host of dwarfs, elves, trolls, and other supernatural sprites who constantly alter human destiny in the most outrageously capricious fashion. An unconscionable range of supernatural power is suggested in the account of Thor's trials of strength in the Hall of the Giants, when the prowess of the most powerful god appears infinitesimal in respect to the tasks that are presented to him. Significantly, he fails in his attempt to drain the drinking horn because of its magical attachment to the ocean that surrounds the earth; he cannot lift the old gray cat because it is the force of gravity; and he is helplessly enfeebled in his wrestling match with the old woman because she personifies old age. All convey the absolute futility of attempting to pit human prowess against the forces of Nature.

Mysterious accessions of power by mortal or semimortal heroes likewise confute the existence of any pattern in the conduct of the universe that is comprehensible to human logic. When Siegfried eats the heart of the dragon Fafnir that he has killed, he attains godlike superiority over ordinary mortals by virtue of his power to communicate with *nature* through understanding the language of the birds and animals. The uncertainty of everything is underlined in northern mythology by the concept of an eventual *Götterdämmerung*, when the gods man knows are defeated by the mysteriously powerful giants, and the universe returns to chaos. In Greek mythology the gods of mankind are expected to *win* the final battle with the giants, as depicted in the gigantomachy of the Great Altar at Pergamon (Plate 4b).

Eighth- and ninth-century Hiberno-Saxon interlace (Plate 20) may be cited as an example of the early northern tendency toward intensely active, structurally complex design of unclear objective reference. Though more than a thousand years later than the classical art of Greece, they must be regarded as the beginning of European cultural expression in the north (previous production that was not provincially dependent on Rome being considered Asiatic or primitive). These devout creations of a newly converted people strikingly display the characteristic anxiety of northern culture in moiling cross pages, illuminated initials and borders, wherein purely linear motifs are woven to and fro, constantly bending back on themselves. Sometimes the lines are merely ribbons; sometimes they are highly convoluted extensions of birds or animals suggesting the animal art of the earlier settlers from the east.

Ethnic influences on plastic expression continue well beyond primitive periods, although the styles of north and south gradually become less completely independent. Even in latter-day painting, some critics suggest, for example, that the dynamic quality of Van Gogh's style derives from his Dutch origin, and that the development of twentieth-century expressionism in Germany is a continuation of early northern mysticism.

Contrasts between the styles of northern and southern Europe are clearly discernible despite the common aims of all cultural expression west, approximately, of the Pripet Marshes from the fifteenth to the seventeenth centuries. In that "age of cities" community patronage tended to shift weight to local rather than ecclesiastical or other international influences on taste, until the "exportation" of the Italian Renaissance to newly important national capitals produced a new internationalism, led in the plastic arts by the taste of the French court.

A painting by the early Flemish artist Jan van Eyck, in contrast with one approximately contemporary by the Florentine Andrea Verrocchio, will show how much more intensely detailed the northern style is, by way of attempting to present the phenomenal complexity of objective vision (Plate 21a and b). Although the forms created in Van Eyck's Ghent Retable, for example, are tactile and distinct, the heavily draped human bodies show less clarified articulation than do the "anatomical" figures of Christ and St. John in Verrocchio's *Baptism of Christ* and other works by the so-called "Florentine Naturalists." Here the artist appears to be analyzing the human figure in an intellectual fashion, proudly recording his newly discovered knowledge of anatomy, whereas in the north heavy or complex drapery draws attention away from considerations of precise bodily structure, as can be seen also in Claes Sluter's imposing figure of Moses (Plate 36b). Northern puritanism is sometimes cited to explain this hesitation about representing the human body; but what would this be, if not the same tension regarding the mysteries of nature?

Background is relatively simple in the Italian proto-Renaissance and even for some time later in the south, with the figures at the picture plane filling the entire area of the composition, and the surrounding landscape, however detailed or extensive, reduced to a kind of theatrical backdrop. In the Van Eyck Retable, on the other hand, the much reduced human figures are placed definitely *in the landscape,* although the composition is quite planimetric, and trees and rocks as well as distant towns, valleys and mountains, are developed with a baffling network of detail, suggesting the complexity of actual vision rather than any clarifying reduction by analysis and selection. The same subject is treated mystically in Van Eyck's *Adoration of the Lamb,* factually in Verrocchio's *Baptism of Christ;* or, in other words, Van Eyck (and his society) accepts the mystery as a fact. Verrocchio can objectify only the historical incident. Both styles are essentially analytical in terms of what come later, but with respect to one another, northern painting shows an affinity for sensational complexity by contrast with the work done at the same time in the south.

A similar contrast between northern and southern styles of the same era appears likewise in later work. Rembrandt (Plate 39b) and Rubens (Plate 41) in the north emerge as tremendously vital and productive exponents of quite different aspects of Baroque or sensational style, from among a host of outstanding Flemish and Dutch seventeenth-century painters, several of whom pushed on to new realizations of light and space (Plate 39a). Italian artists of the period, however, seemed to hold back in the development of some aspects of sensational style, and Caravaggio was the only outstanding Baroque painter of Italy to develop a completely optic treatment of form. A Caracci (Plate 2b), or a Reni obviously clings to patterns of classical clarity in modeling the human figure. Although there is considerable recessional movement in the form of melodramatic *contrapposto* and minor figures at the picture plane pushing the main focus back into depth, there is frequently also a suggestion of plane in the alternation of light and dark masses to define deep space. In Rembrandt's compositions, however, the figures move into depth in a natural recession, and are felt to be surrounded by a perfectly continuous volume of space. His landscapes and landscape backgrounds recede to the horizon with a sense of complete natural continuity, and this is true generally of landscape painting in the north, even to some extent as early as that of Pieter Breughel the Elder.

Intangible space and light are indeed the thoroughly sensational material of Rembrandt's painting. The handsome volume of his figures registers on human attention as sensuously appealing materials—flesh, fur, deep-piled textiles or bright metal—rather than as precisely described bulks. Light and recessional movement in monumental seventeenth-century Italian painting, on the other hand, are merely introduced as dramatizing embellishments of crowded but clearly enumerated *dramatis personae,* whose delineation displays a virtuoso's catalogue of the precepts of academic drawing.

Rubens' intensely dramatic style, outstripping the Baroque quality of Italian masters with whom he was associated in his years of study and professional beginnings in Italy, may be due to a particular vitality or tension derived from his native Flemish cultural environment (Plate 41). At any rate it exhibits the affinity of northern culture for the extremes of sensational development in style, which is so marked also in the late development of Gothic architecture in Germany and England (Plate 19a).

After Rubens there is no longer such a great distinction between northern and southern styles, and European art, centering in Paris at least in its more self-conscious aspects, tends to break more sharply on lines of aristocratic versus bourgeois taste. Rubens in a sense is the last northern painter and the first international one in modern times. For his style embodies clearly the influence of his training in Italy and was universally acclaimed throughout the royal courts of Europe.

## THE PROCESS OF CULTURAL EVOLUTION

Day-to-day struggle with primitive nature obviously has little or no direct impact on basic cultural attitudes today. Several thousands of years ago, after countless generations in which a prime consideration of any social unit was the fear of complete destruction by famine, pestilence, or other natural catastrophe, various means of security were devised, and the virtual subjugation of nature may be said to have taken place. Group labor either by voluntary association or various forms of bondage; extensive marketing and commercial relations; gradual development of reliable agricultural techniques have provided since the beginning of recorded history a degree of social continuity and material surplus beyond the requirement for subsistence, enabling at least some levels of the population to envision for themselves a relative degree of security. It became possible for the community to support an increasingly large and specialized group of craftsmen continuously from generation to generation, who thus were enabled to develop techniques providing further defense against nature in the form of adequate, and later elaborate, forms of clothing and shelter. Ideals of abundance, personal independence, elegance, and the like dawned on the human horizon to supplant the fearsome emphasis on mere survival.

Thus the primitive struggle against nature diminished in importance as an influence on human culture, although the basic ideology of order versus mystery to which it gave rise continued to characterize the feelings and beliefs of mankind. The original impression of the struggle was deep and powerful, and the forces of nature can still be imposing even when held at a distance by human ingenuity. Furthermore, the distance did not suddenly become as great as it may seem today, especially in northern Europe where extensive tracts of land remained undeveloped by man through the Middle Ages. Provision of food and fuel for each following winter was a major technical problem to a vast number of individuals

until the industrial era; and virtually no objective explanation of cosmological phenomena was accessible to the general public. However, other
influences on style developed as natural environment ceased to be the
dominant preoccupation, and after the seventeenth century it may be
said that the ethnic or geoclimatic factor is infinitesimal except perhaps
for some forms of nationalistic retrospection.

European culture for at least the last thousand years has been in almost
constant flux at an ever accelerating pace. The clearest and most continuous picture of this change may be viewed in the plastic arts, which
reveal a pattern of growth following a course, similar in each distinct
culture, from a stage that clearly displays the analytical stylistic characteristics to one showing the sensational group. In other words, it immediately appears that the polar categories of style bear an evolutionary
relation to one another. The development of Attic Greek severity into
the complex virtuosity of the Hellenistic style may thus be compared
with a similar evolution from the staid clarity of Renaissance forms to
the exuberance of the Baroque by a procedure more apt and illuminating than the mere interchange of labels, and without derogatory reference
to the "loss" of certain values which ignores their replacement by others.

*The Biological Fallacy.* The appearance of a cultural cycle or trend
in the direction indicated has commonly been explained by what Geoffrey
Scott in his *Architecture of Humanism* called the "biological fallacy"—
the notion that a culture, like a plant or animal, passes through periods
of growth, maturity and decay of commensurate span. The style of the
middle period, by analogy with the presumably superior powers of a
creature in the "prime of life" is deemed finer than the others. Thus the
production of archaic periods and primitive cultures has often been
scorned as inept, while both Hellenistic and Baroque styles have been
damned as "decadent" despite an obvious vitality in no way suggesting
the decrepit stages of senility and impending death.

As an analogy with cultural evolution the usual pattern of infancy,
maturity and senescence is oversimplified and misleading in the implication of complete homogeneity and equal duration for each stage.
As Heinrich Wölfflin points out in his *Principles of Art History,* man
considers the blossom to be the highest product of the rosebush, but
favors the fruit of its cousin the apple tree. Different phases of maturity
in the vegetable world are selected as they happen to suit human purpose.
Plato's description of the ideal series of social functions in the career
of a citizen of his *Republic* indicates compensating values of vigor and

experience ranging from youth to age. Regarding classic and baroque types of style as analogous to these differing stages in the prime of life dispels prejudice against one or the other based on its evolutionary position. Ineptitudes that might be related to extremes of infancy and decay are properly reduced to brief stages of unimportant production.

Cultural creation of the first rank is always the accomplishment of mature, capable, aware, and superior persons. Obviously Botticelli and Leonardo in the "youth" of the Renaissance were master craftsmen, personally as adult as Bernini or anyone else in its decadence or "old age." Each stage has a characteristic value: early periods a penetrating ingenuity, late periods a suavity and technical command that compare favorably with one another and with the transitional or "Golden Age" styles often distinct from both.

Accepting the premise that art is expression, no one can advocate a single universal taste for evaluation of all styles. Presumably first-rate art of any period comes close to expressing the society for which it was created, and the most significant value to be derived from analyzing the great art of the past lies in the clarification of this relationship.

*Sequential Relation of the Polar Categories.* Just as analytical or sensational expression appears to be favored broadly in the respective spheres of northern European and Mediterranean culture, so is it also found to characterize respectively the earlier and later phases of a given cultural evolution. It can readily be indicated that the problems of evolving creative techniques cause a tendency to analytical form in the beginning. But what accounts for the impulse to go on and produce sensational expression once a satisfactory analytical style has been accomplished? Given the rise of a sensational style with its characteristic charm and brilliance, why does cultural revolution generally reject such superiority and revive the more staid rhythm and clarity of the analytical approach?

It has frequently been noted that the style of an artist early in his career is "tight," linear, stiff, and that he "loosens up" later on (Plate 24). Likewise as a given society evolves, its basic motivations change, energetic enterprise typical of a pioneering era gives way to luxurious sophistication as power is established and leadership centralized. Nowhere is this reflected more clearly than in the stylistic evolution of the plastic arts, nor can art be understood without consideration of the stage or attitude of the society it was produced to serve.

There are cultures to which the application of this method of analysis appears at first glance to be impossible or less rewarding than in constantly changing Western Europe where historical stages seem to be so much more distinct than in other times and places. However, there is considerable indication that the art of the great ancient and Eastern cultures, though more static, may be analyzed in similar terms. Painting in China, for example, shows quite clearly a stylistic evolution from analytical generality in the linear style of Ku K'ai-chih to the particularized and sensational styles of later naturalism, though embracing a much longer span than similar evolutions in the West. In other areas the lack of change reflects the absence of such forces as account for stylistic evolution in European art. The fact that change does not occur in art, the stage at which development is arrested, and similar considerations, will expose or illustrate significant aspects of the cultures in question.

Some attempt has been made above to connect the polar categories of style in art with the way in which certain types of person tend to operate in their daily lives. It has been a commonplace of man's observations of his fellow man almost as far back as literature records them that a pattern of conduct or "personality" characterizes the acts of any given individual, from the way he wears his hat or walks across the room, to his reactions under the severest personal stress. "The *crafty* Ulysses," the contrasting roughness of Esau and gentleness of Isaac, current stereotypes of the "typical" businessman, politician, suburbanite, and many others, indicate that a close relation exists between an individual's conduct and some basic aspect of a personality which in turn is related to his background of experience and his role in the community.

Similar "personalities" characterize the cultures of various times and places throughout history. A fantastic and licentious type of gaiety can be associated with the latter days of the French monarchy, a more pompous and perhaps brutal grandeur with the height of absolute power in Italy during the seventeenth century, political and commercial ingenuity with the rise of the Renaissance in Florence.

Such a cultural personality becomes basic and characteristic of a people as a result of objective conditions governing their joint survival and fortunes. In order to know why style in art moves from analytical to sensational form, it is necessary simply to discover what forces impel the artist and the society in which he lives to change from an analytical to a sensational approach to the conduct of life. There are two types of force producing such change (conditioned by constant regional tendencies), one applying to the artist personally in the development of his craft, which might be called "technological" motivation, the other in the broader field of social attitudes and institutions which might be called "socioeconomic" motivation of stylistic change. The next step in this discussion, then, is to describe the process whereby technological factors in the development of craft, and socioeconomic factors in the growth of human culture may bring about changes of style from one of the polar categories to the other. The former of these influences is more elementary though less important, and should therefore be considered first.

### THE ARTIST AND HIS CRAFT—TECHNOLOGICAL MOTIVATION

Just as the struggles of mankind with environments of different degrees of difficulty result in cultures based on various attitudes toward the significance of order in the natural universe, so the artist's own struggle with his medium forces him to rely at first on an orderly, analytical approach to the creative problem, which may be relaxed to permit sensational fusion and elaboration only in the later stages, if there is any pressure in that direction on the part of the community as a whole or its patronizing group. There have been two outstanding periods in the history of Western art when technological factors seem to have contributed to the analytical appearance of early work as compared with the more sensational quality of subsequent style, namely, the early stages of Greek art, and the time when realistic interests were being revived for the Renaissance. In addition, each artist personally must traverse a similar period in his own career of professional development, varying in depth and magnitude according to current practices of training, as will be discussed. An understanding of technological influence on style is necessary also for the proper interpretation of provincial art.

Examination of Greek sculpture from its beginnings in the archaic period through its entire course to the late Hellenistic, shows a related succession of styles which seem to depend to some extent on a growing technical ability to achieve the constant, basic end of an idealized natural verisimilitude. The rigidity of the early "Apollo" or *kouros* figures (Plate 22a), drastic limitation of action in the pose, tentative and gradual achievement of inner contours throughout the archaic period, all seem to indicate difficulty for the sculptor in controlling his material and in creating exactly the form he visualized. Rapid growth toward constantly more naturalistic appearance shows that the earlier styles must have been limited in some degree by incomplete know-how.

The importance of archaic style as naturalistic expression in its own time must not be discounted. To some extent the lack of optic reality so much missed now and in the recent past, is considerably compensated by the tactile reality of the simplified, powerful forms; and the bright coloring that has largely disappeared from long-buried surfaces further enhanced the aesthetic experience. In a primitive situation even an archaic Apollo represented a long step toward imitation of nature, probably deemed an ideal impossible of perfect or even approximate accomplishment, indeed close to magic. The need for expression was then a genuine hunger, not a critical appetite, and the most serviceable achievements were gladly accepted. Technical limitations are clearly reflected in the character of the finished product, but their importance as a complete and derogatory explanation of archaic style has been considerably overemphasized in academic criticism.

The Greek sculptor was working for a society that had faith in the capacity as well as the destiny of mankind to control its environment, and therefore he constantly sought more satisfactory solutions. Each generation respected its own taste and accepted any change it found satisfactory. Though revered, ancient work was not so completely canonized as to block further development. For the Greek artist did not occupy the perhaps enviable position of the artist in primitive cultures, where he was considered a magical communicant with cosmic forces, and his production immutable as divine revelation. In Greece, he was given the task of portraying nature ideally, and though his earlier archaic production was accepted, there was a constant pressure to move closer to the then still distant goal. Conventions for representing complex details like the anatomy of an eye, a hand or a knee were tentatively accepted for use over a period of time, but change was welcomed and is clearly observable from decade to decade (Plate 22).

When the Greek artist had fabricated a suitable image to serve as focus for the cultural expression of his society, however, his task was not over. Early in the fifth century B.C., several decades before the beginning of the Periclean era in Athens, Greek art seems to have reached its goal. Although governed by highly canonical formulations of what was considered the ideal of human beauty, and characterized by a sharpness of definition that is rare in human vision, there is no sense of distortion or ignorance of structure in a work like the *Spearbearer* of

Polykleitos (Plate 16a) or the sculptured decorations of the Parthenon. The forms became convincing to the eye as well as the hand. Yet they remain quite linear in clarity of contour, structure and detail. Compositions, just beginning to be attempted at this time, are closed and planimetric, both in recognition of the actual plane of the material base and in the omission of any reference to spatial environment.

Even the revered accomplishments of the Periclean Age are not the last word in Greek naturalism, however. In the fourth century and in the Hellenistic period, Greek artists finally achieve an expression of the variety, complexity, motility and passion that seems more a reflection of life than an analytical commentary upon it (Plates 4b and 16b). Though this final stage is not intrinsically superior to the previous one, its accomplishment required the development of certain purely technological advance, which could not be made before the earlier development had taken place. In the Italian Renaissance, when similar technological problems were involved in the evolution of style, it is interesting to note how far in advance of its greatest technical achievements their aims were recognized. Leonardo was greatly concerned with illumination and movement, though his style is essentially analytical. Massaccio displays passages of archaic simplicity, despite his sophisticated objectives of optic and recessional representation. Indeed, a bare *statement* of the aims of compositional fusion and spatial illusion is legible even as early as the work of Giotto.

Convincing visual representation of natural objects requires a deep understanding of their structure and constituent shapes, for the complexity and intimate fusion of parts in a living organism is not readily encompassed by the mechanical analysis of human logic. Though people are quite familiar in a sense with the forms that surround them, so that deformity, monstrosities or even individual peculiarity is readily recognized, most of the knowledge of environment is retained in their hands rather than in their eyes, and initial attempts to represent even the most highly generalized types are quite far from natural appearance. By laborious analysis of the object, by checking and rechecking obvious discrepancies in what the artist has made with how it really looks, a series of formulae may be developed through sustained study by professional persons whereby the desired aim of natural appearance is approximated.

The extent to which human understanding of physical environment is basically tactile rather than optic is an endless source of surprise when demonstrated to anyone today. The question arises whether it is possible that the human eye may have evolved its present efficiency later than the completion of man's other senses. It can be answered also, however, by the increased emphasis on consumer functions giving rise to increasingly sensational cultural expressions in modern society, to be discussed later.

The process of careful study by which the change from archaic massiveness to increasingly optical realism is accomplished is obviously analytical in essence, and accordingly at the outset it produces a result that coincides with the analytical category of style. A painting or sculpture will have the appearance of being pieced together from a number of individually studied parts. As a result of concentration on the basic character of the forms, they will be clearly defined, with firm, continuous contours. What has been called "frontality" in the typically archaic figure, each part facing directly forward with no twist or swing to left or right on the vertical axis, or for that matter, any other movement of the major parts of the body, is an elementary form of planimetric spatial construction. The archaic attitude was indeed so literal plastically that no thought of space was involved at all. It is a sort of pre-illusionistic stage in art, rated by some critics as not art at all, in which no optic imitation whatsoever was conceived, but only a purely plastic or tactile substitution. If the subject calls for any combination of figures, they will be studied individually, spread out with little or no overlapping, and this will confer a planimetric quality on whatever spatial composition is attempted. Any indication of environment will also adhere strictly to the plane, but background will be largely suppressed in recognition of the actual surface of the material base. The figures on Wedgwood china, for example (developed in the neoclassic period as a reflection of classic Greek relief sculpture like the inner frieze of the Parthenon) or the Altar of Aphrodite (Plate 4a), are composed as a frank application to the surface of a vessel rather than attempting to create any illusion of depth. Details or inner contours in the earliest work are reduced to a minimum. and in two-dimensional composition, forms and parts of forms tend to be faced so that the most significant silhouette parallels the picture plane, as in the profile or medallion portraits of the fifteenth century in Italy. Thus early stages show a clear correspondence with the various aspects of the analytical category, due in great part to the need for the artist to concentrate his attention analytically on various phases of his difficult and unfamiliar craft problem.

As understanding of basic aspects of the human figure is achieved, a canon or formula is evolved which the artist may learn and repeat with comparative facility. His creative procedure (in view of the demands for constantly greater sophistication that have been made upon him in Western culture) then becomes virtually an *intuitive* application of indoctrinated formulae to the observed *phenomenal appearance* or sensations of reality. The individual parts of the figure become associated in a less mechanical or patterned fashion, articulations are more fluid and subtle, the combination of parts more truly organic. The figure, in short, is unified. Then it is made to move and assume various postures implying action within a limited volume of surrounding space. Further unification in groups with other figures is evolved, and a similar process obtains in the development of an increasingly complex, fused and recessional representation of environment.

Each of these developments in a sense is the growth of art upon itself, not directly upon its natural subject material. For technological reasons alone, though of course there were others, Giotto could not have painted the Sistine ceiling as Michelangelo did, much less a Tiepolo ceiling. Not only could he not have foreseen the possibility of such complete fulfillment of the aims in art that he was seeking to express, but physical indoctrination of his hand and eye with so many overlays of discovery and reapplication of new formulae could not have been accomplished in one lifetime. For artistic skill is not a matter of intellectual knowledge that can be committed to memory from a book, but something that must be worked out in repeated and time-consuming experience.

*Model vs. Memory Image.* "Why didn't they just look at a model?" is a common question regarding archaic style, especially Greek, where the naturalistic ideal seemed to be well recognized from the beginning. The first answer to that is, of course, if they had, they would still have seen in it the same analytical generalizations. However, it is the natural tendency for people to draw at first from "memory images" the mental picture one retains of familiar objects or types of object. Such a memory image is a composite of all previous visual *and tactile* experience with a given form. Varied and fleeting images of the object in movement, under changes of light, or other phenomenal qualities necessarily cancel out. Hence the memory image has a distinctly analytical character, which is actually preferable in certain cultural contexts.

The universal tendency to work at first from a memory image may be easily accounted for. Everyone feels he is quite familiar with the common objects of everyday life. It is therefore entirely logical for the primitive artist to suppose that, having gazed upon human figures thousands or hundreds of thousands of times, one more look would be of little additional value, and this is true in terms of what he would be looking for.

Latter-day study of the model and *plein aire* landscape painting are in a sense the application in art of the methods of scientific investigation, or the submission of human understanding to the complexity of natural phenomena. Though taken for granted today, experimentation is quite a sophisticated intellectual procedure, long unthought of even by scientists; and the parallel in art of observing actual models likewise could not arise until an advanced stage of cultural development. Actually, of course, placing an easel in front of a landscape or nude model may involve very little genuine analysis, but rather an opportunity for the artist to record the purely subjective aesthetic sensations he experiences.

Another confusion tending unjustly to disparage the accomplishment of early styles is the tendency to think of painting and sculpture as *visual* arts, referring simply to optical experience, whereas they are based equally or even more on the human capacity for tactile and kinaesthetic sensation of masses and space. That is to say, the bulk of a statue may be felt by looking without lifting, but such meaning is for the muscles, not the eye. The same is true of the *implied* bulk of a figure in a painting. The inability to represent natural appearance in early styles is associated with this prior interest in bulk. As the evolution toward the sensational pole develops, artists soon find the ability to create optically convincing representation of the subject with which they are concerned.

*Examples from the Italian Renaissance.* Technological considerations influence the development of style toward one or the other of the polar categories, not only in a culture which starts with little or no technical competence and cultural tradition, as Greek art appears to have done in its archaic period (despite some remote carry-over from Aegaean and perhaps Egyptian sources), but also when major changes in cultural orientation impose profound redirections on the artist in his expressive aims. When new social perspectives indicate objectives outside the range of his traditional procedures, however sophisticated his art may have become in terms of other, earlier interests, he must then consciously adapt his creative skills to this new purpose. Again the procedure of analyzing and logically correlating means and ends must be used, and the analytical qualities of form inevitably appear in the resulting product. The second of the two outstanding periods in Western culture when technological factors become an important influence on style is the brilliant development of the Renaissance in Italy, crowning the Age of Cities.

At the end of the early medieval period a new humanism arose, most consciously recognized as such in the cultural centers of Italy. It was inspired by the abundance of material comforts and new opportunities for the individual to be found in the burgeoning market economy. For its expression, the artists were required to invent a new realism to replace the "other-worldly" stylizations of Byzantine art. The ideal of a complete naturalism was so far from the Byzantine formulations in which Italian artists were trained through the fourteenth century, that much genuinely pioneering invention was required. Changes in material were comparatively slight, fresco for murals and tempera on wood for panel painting continuing to predominate. Mosaic was dropped and oil was gradually adopted later on. It was the struggle with basically unfamiliar problems of representation that led to much of the thoroughly analytical expression of the new style, culminating in a linear naturalism of the most thoroughly clarified and tactile forms that have ever been presented in painting. The stated admiration of the period for naturalistic and dynamic effects might be expected to produce a more sensational quality, which eventually did appear in the Baroque period; but the static, conceptual quality of the analytical approach enforced by the technical problems asserted itself with inevitable priority. This divergence of object and result is perhaps most clear in the work of Paolo Uccello, whose elaborate perspective structures are quite planimetric, and whose violently active horses in the battle pictures seem to be cast solid and absolutely immobile in their curious poses, although they were obviously intended to convey so much action (Plate 11a).

In Botticelli's *Primavera* (Plate 23) all the figures, but most noticeably perhaps the one at the left in the group of the Three Graces, are made up of a series of details brilliantly described by a clear, insistent outline, but the exaggerated movement of the figure's posture seen as a whole is unconvincing or lacking in the graceful flow of terpsichorean movement that was intended. These artists had not had time, in a manner of speaking, to discover that in art the whole can be greater than the sum of its parts; or in terms of the present analysis, the early analytical approach led to a mechanical articulation of parts rather than the organic fusion that might have suited their intentions much better. The lack of fusion does not reduce the brilliance of the drawing in these figures, which were created and may be observed with successive attention to part after part (as described on page 43 ff.) but detracts only from the naturalness of the total effect. Mechanically articulated works of this sort make up in the length of time they may freshly support the spectator's attention what they lack in the amount of material integrated for simultaneous grasp as in the later, technically more sophisticated sensational styles. These are of course the respective values characteristically offered by the polar categories, and each is thoroughly acceptable only to someone who is sympathetic in his personal character or cultural orientation to the analytical or sensational expression that is conveyed.

Later in the Renaissance the phenomenon of a stylistic evolution within the career of a single artist is first clearly to be seen. This would not occur noticeably in the case of an artist who attacked the creative problem merely as a craftsman, producing a given type of object according to established formulae. However, there were those who attempted to carry their professional practice ever closer to the rapidly projected ideals of the time. Their objective in each work was not only to raise it to a given standard, but to advance contemporary standards as well.

In such a career, the earlier and later phases show the same tendencies of development from analytical to sensational form as does the evolution of the entire culture. The artist moves from the studious stiffness of an early analytical stage to a gradually more accomplished fluidity, by an increase in skill through indoctrination of his muscles and senses. The emergence of such a late style is clearly recognizable in the careers of artists like Titian (compare Plate 24a and b), El Greco, Velasquez and Rembrandt, as well as the more modern figures of Turner, Monet, Inness, Renoir and many others. Sometimes called "fuzzy, impressionistic, painterly," these are sensational styles evolved as the artist gradually brings his technical skill up to the stated ideals of a sophisticated period.

In some cases, if the master lives long enough, his skill eventually carries these ideals to an unanticipated extreme, to a refinement *beyond* the sophistication of all but a few of his contemporaries. This is frequently the actual situation of the so-called "artist ahead of his time." By concentrating to an extreme degree on the professional or aesthetic sophistication of his product, he loses contact with the human interests of his society, which is the only reliable basis for a wide audience. Subsequent appreciation is not due to a "catching up" of popular taste, but to the fact that in later generations, when the work is removed from concrete social involvement or responsibility in museums or other collections of antiquities, it is then judged only by connoisseurs on aesthetic

grounds. The antecedents of the same connoisseurs doubtless appreci-
ated the work in its own time, for there are records of "faithful" patrons
in most cases; but their opinions could not prevail against a public un-
willing to accept aesthetic sophistication in place of other, more vital
or obvious values.

*Problems of Training.* The complexity of sensational styles poses
special problems in the training of succeeding generations of artists. As
long as a style remains analytical, advances in technique modify or supplant previous forms and the artist has a comparatively direct, uncomplicated objective. However, the evolution of a sensational attitude
must be based upon the more elementary formulations which may not
be discarded, although they may recede eventually into virtual oblivion.
Archaic Greek sculptors for many years made an eye with lids that were
simple arcs. At a certain point it was noticed that the curve of the eyelid
was uneven, the upper rising higher inside the center, the lower lid
dipping lower outside the center, and the earlier convention was simply
replaced. But when sensational style caused the outlines to be softened
to provide a sense of the texture of flesh as in the work of Praxiteles,
deepened for dramatic effect as in the manner of Skopas, or turned to
suggest spatial recession in relief sculpture, these subtleties of modeling
and perspective had to be superimposed on the basic formula. Because
a sensational style grows through successive overlays of technical modification, it may be advisable to train the new generation of artists by means
of a series of steps repeating the process of its historical development from
analytical antecedents, instead of aiming directly at the eventually desired complication.

During the high Renaissance in Italy and in some subsequent periods
modeled thereon, the process of natural representation was studied more
or less analytically in drawing from nude models, copying of earlier
works, studying isolated bits of drapery, muscular anatomy, the skeleton,
and in exercises in perspective. A regime of rigorous indoctrination was
required of the prospective artist, as in any other professional or intellectual field. In fact, at one time the training to be an artist was undoubtedly
the most exacting and inclusive of all the professions.

Drawings made for purposes of this type of study tend to be stiffer and
more linear, i.e., more analytical, than the fully developed professional
style of any given period or of the artist's own eventual style. Attempts
to create drawings or finished works in a complex sensational style without sufficient or appropriate training produce inferior results which are

easily distinguished. On the one hand, imperfect integration of parts, "hardness" of detail, stiffness of movement, impart a relatively analytical character which is in conflict with the fluid dynamic effect obviously intended, somewhat as in provincial style, to be examined later. Where the fluid appearance is achieved without sufficient training in elementary components, it will be found to lack depth or substance, as a mere "drawing of a drawing," to use a phrase of the late Kenneth Hayes Miller. This indicates clearly that to achieve the maximum values of sensational style, analytical experience of some sort should come first in the training of the individual artist as it does in the total cultural development.

The virtue of basing sensational style on analytical antecedents exposes an important fallacy in contemporary teaching of art to prospective professional artists. On the one hand, "progressive" art schools eliminate early stages of purely technical training as "academic" and limiting to the creative personality, for which they substitute an emphasis on free development of individual expression. Not only does this risk the loss of positive content in the program, but it allows the immature person who is attracted to a career in art on the basis of its romantic aspects in modern society, to avoid necessary formative pressures. An atmosphere results that may handicap serious students by a relaxation of discipline and neglect of adequate technical instruction.

On the other hand, academic schools may prescribe training exercises merely as superficial familiarization with an advanced goal, copying from masterpieces or from models, and memorizing formulae mechanically with little genuine understanding of their dynamic significance. Examples for study like the casts used in the standard "Antique" class, tend to be selected from the most highly developed, sensational periods. The students produce mere *pastiches* involving only the slightest amount of basic understanding and creative force. This procedure indoctrinates the student only with the *appearance* of sensational expression so that it may be imitated, failing to engender an intuitive integration of the skills developed by earlier analysis. Beginning rather with analytical study and representation, perhaps copying works from earlier stages, emphasizing line and structure rather than light and shade in drawing, would provide the neophyte with a basis for deeper and more genuine understanding of his means of expression, even if he is to create eventually in a sensational style.

The alternative is not between working and not working, for a student may be required laboriously and exactly to copy the patches of light and

shade, or "values" as they are frequently called, on a plaster cast of the
Belvedere torso, *Laocoön,* or one of the figures from Michelangelo's
Medici Tombs for a year or two, and to repeat the process for a similar
period with the nude and draped model, without ever having learned
anything about the detailed structure and articulation of the figure. If
the recapitulation of analytical solutions is thus dropped from professional training as a style moves into its sensational stage, the insubstanti-
ality of a rococo or an impressionistic style results. If some analytical
basis is maintained, the vigorous expression of a Golden Age may be
produced.

*Identifying the Creative Personality.* Examination of influences on
style resulting from the technological struggle of the individual artist,
yields some insight regarding personal aptitudes for the profession. The
creative role during a period of analytical expression would require an
intensely practical type, coming to grips with materials and problems
of his craft, pulling things apart to see how they work, then putting
them together to make something new in a reasoned, methodical manner.
The role of the artist creating in an analytical style is that of a clear-
headed, confident and informed craftsman, who knows how to go about
what he is attempting to do, or, how to figure it out, if the problem at
hand is a bit strange. This is a rather different sort of person from the
undisciplined, inspirational bohemian who is popularly supposed to be
the "creative type" today; but Pollaiuolo, Leonardo da Vinci, Titian,
Breughel, to mention only a few of the most obvious, were certainly
practical, inquiring personalities, and two early American painters,
Samuel F. B. Morse and Robert Fulton, each produced and promoted
epoch-making mechanical inventions.

Sensational styles, on the other hand, derive from a fluent familiarity
with technical means invented by forerunners; they require a degree of
connoisseurship or sophistication in art, and are impatient with elementary details; they exploit sensation, novelty, syncopation, elliptical
reference of many sorts, played upon familiar formulations inherited
from a long cultural development. The previous existence of formulae
or ideals upon which these types of "switch" are superimposed indicates
clearly that sensational style may occur only in an advanced stage of a
culture.

The personality of the artist in this stage may be somewhat warped by
the intensive process of mastering a considerable heritage of skills and
images developed in previous ages. He is often forced to neglect the

practical world outside his studio, a world which is so highly organized economically that it requires some degree of functional specialization throughout all ranks of society; his character takes on the apparently impractical, self-centered, socially bizarre appearance of the typical virtuoso. Other factors contribute also to this distortion of the artist's role in a sophisticated stage of cultural evolution, especially in the romantic atmosphere of the recent past; but the requirements of technological mastery, including expert refinement of taste, play their part, contributing the most dignified element of motivation for the so-called "eccentricities of genius."

The same process takes place, of course, in less colorful fashion, among practitioners of many other professions, who must likewise specialize intently in small segments of a highly complex technology or economic structure, which tends to blur a broader understanding of the world they live in. Since the majority of trades and professions cannot be considered glamorous, however, as for some reason the arts seem to be, there is little point in calling attention to the role of butcher or accountant, for example, by appropriate eccentricities. In fact, any posturing on the part of tradesmen and professionals must be rather in the direction of asserting their probity and practical effectiveness.

Glamorizing of cultural activity has attracted to the arts a vast number of practitioners for other than genuine professional concerns. The resulting flood of overproduction has created a competitive situation in which many artists feel that eccentricities of personal conduct, as well as of the style in which they create, must be exaggerated as much as possible to attract attention and attest to the intensity of their genius.

Any tendency of artistically creative people to function in an apparently undirected "inspirational" chaos is at best a concomitant of one pole of cultural expression. The tendency for artists to show certain deviations from common practice depended originally on the quantity of technical material, the degree of virtuosity they had to master to be able to practice in their specialized field, and by the extent to which they were required to concentrate on the accomplishments of the past, with their own creative ingenuity given over to sensational modifications of an established tradition. They were interpreting art itself rather than life, and their esoteric dedication engendered oddities of manner that were increasingly imitated by poseurs and pretenders.

The analytical personality of an early, formative stage of culture is more profoundly creative in the sense that he must solve problems by a fresh understanding of means in relation to ends; whereas the later artist acquires accepted solutions of basic problems and "invents" only novel accents and reinterpretations. One is essentially ingenious in a pioneer or revolutionary sense; the other is essentially a follower, his ingenuity consisting in reapplications, increasingly subtle and difficult perhaps, but involving only slight twists or sorties from familiar trails, rather than any fundamental redirection.

It is for this reason that "infant prodigies" are most characteristic of late periods, when a sensational style is well established. In recent times, a number of children have contributed remarkably capable performances as actors and instrumental musicians, because these are two fields in which elaborate techniques have become established by consistent development for some time past. There is much to be *learned,* little to be *worked out,* a task which would be beyond the capacity of an inexperienced child. Similarly, at the end of the Renaissance, it was possible for the drawings of Giovanni Lorenzo Bernini as a boy of twelve, having been schooled in the elaborate conventions of representing the human figure by his father, to impress the Vatican court as a child prodigy.

These remarks on the quality of creative personality interpreted from a technological point of view are not intended as any disparagement of the role or personality of the genuine artist in a late or sensational stage. Some consideration is required simply to redress a common assumption, at least in the arts, that unless a person is in some way "colorful," impulsive, peremptory, and generally undisciplined, he cannot be very "creative." More damaging in some ways is the converse, that the work of anyone willing to outrage accepted standards of conduct to a sufficient degree must be given serious consideration as very profound art.

*Limits of Technical Influence on Style.* The discussion of the influence on style of the artist's personal struggle with his own professional problems has covered a wide range of topics. A summary of the phases discussed will provide an opportunity for citing certain cautions, and will establish a bridge to further consideration of evolutionary influences on style. It has been seen that artists faced with basic problems of developing their craft, either in a primitive situation or in a period of fundamental cultural reorientation, are forced to adopt a probing, analytical approach which imprints the familiar linear, planimetric and closed form on their compositions.

As the attention of the artist is released from concern with minutiae by the establishment of a basic vocabulary of form, the potentialities of a more fused, sensational expression begin to flower insofar as there may be pressure for change. Thus sensational expression is evidence of an advanced technical development because its characteristic fusion of form requires the artist to control all parts of the design in simultaneous consideration. To do this he must have a sure familiarity with the constituent elements. The scope of human attention is greatly enhanced in dealing with familiar material, because it may then reach out beyond particular factors and concentrate on a complex totality. Such semiconscious, reflexive or sweeping control of familiar components is essentially an intuitive process, made possible by sufficient prior development and indoctrination to establish the necessary familiarity with fundamentals.

As it will be seen from further analysis of the motivations of style, technological influences have a limited importance in explaining the style of a period. Analytical factors can only be ascribed to such influence when a culture begins with an objective beyond the immediate capacities of its artists. The development of a sensational style does not necessarily follow unless some aspect of the culture makes this type of expression apt. Primitive societies and those that have retained feudal structures over extensive periods of time, like the great river valley civilizations of Egypt and the East, may simply refine and elaborate traditionally their earliest formulations, perpetuating analytical, linear styles in art through ages that produce highly developed sophistication in other phases of the lives of their rulers.

The artist's personal attitude is of course highly dependent on that of the age in which he lives. His adherence in any culture or period to one or the other of the stylistic poles, however greatly it might be influenced by what he thought he *could or could not do,* is equally dependent on what the artist *wanted to do;* which consciously or not is what certain sections of society *want him to do.* Motivations to be dealt with in the succeeding discussion of socioeconomic influences fall predominantly in this area.

### THE ARTIST AND HIS SOCIETY—SOCIOECONOMIC MOTIVATION

Man's reaction to his struggle with natural environment has been seen to exert a basic general influence on style in the direction of one of the poles described or the other. The struggle of the artist to develop his craft has been seen to affect the evolutionary tendencies of growth from the analytical to the sensational qualities of form. By far the most important motivation of change in human culture, however, is the struggle of man to develop and control the community through which the aims of society are sought. These may be called "socioeconomic" factors, and they provide the most extensive explanation of the forms of plastic expression in Western Europe during historic times generally, and the complexities of modern expression in particular.

The great contribution of European capitalism to the physical comfort and spiritual stimulation of mankind has been the element of individual opportunity characteristic of the free market, which is culturally its most positive and crucial aspect. A market economy tends to relate all the property of the community in a framework of the utmost flexibility so that there may be no limit to the scope of a superior individual, nor to the premium that may be earned by his initiative, his ability to make new lands and new processes profitable, to "make the most" of what he has. From this element of opportunity has resulted a social ideology highly concerned with the possibility of change, not only as the hope of the ambitious but as a threat to the laggard and weak. Whereas change had cataclysmic implications for mankind in a primitive economy, today it seems good. Curious and hopeful thousands rush to buy the new gadget, an "under new management" sign is hailed as a harbinger of brilliant advance.

In contrary fashion, societies which were based on static systems of function and reward according to caste, as in Egypt and the Orient, have not exhibited the same constant tendency to change. Value and reverence were accorded predominantly to that which was oldest, with cultural production dedicated to the emulation of tradition and the continuity of familiar forms, although occasional changes came about as the result of specific historical influences, like the personality of Ikhnaton in Egypt, or the conquest of that country by Alexander the Great.

At the close of the prehistoric period in Europe, with the development of comparatively reliable social techniques of production, shelter, commerce and military defense, the strategic center of the struggle for existence moved from the natural to the economic front. Survival depended not so much on the primitive skills of individual self-defense and of wresting sustenance from the wilderness, as on a person's ability to make a socially acceptable contribution in a more specialized way to an organized community. Dependence of the individual on the community increased with the degree of specialization, but the resulting increase in productive efficiency of the economy as a whole compensated the participants with a share in the production of others, providing a better and more secure way of life than they could provide for themselves. In the degree that an individual was thus bound to the interests of his fellow men, he was freed from thralldom to his immemorial struggle against nature for survival. As the scope of his allegiance broadened, from the family, to the clan, to the village, city and state, his potential freedom was increased. It is this observation, among others, to be sure, that inspires so many people at present to strive for the goal of complete global coordination.

Security in the bosom of the community was not the only result of increased efficiency dependent upon the growth of specialization and organization. Those same accomplishments which reduced the fear of various natural hazards—frost, drought, pestilence, storm and consequent famine—soon increased material surpluses beyond the provision of a mere insurance reserve of food supply, and were dedicated increasingly to the creation of comfort and luxury according to the desires of the particular society. It is in this area, in the extra effort expended to make the necessities attractive, demonstrative, imposing as well as functional, that those cultural attitudes may be read which convey the governing ideologies of any society.

*Leadership and the Distribution of Wealth.* A necessary element of coordination among men is leadership, and society has always accorded to its leaders a greater share in social distribution than is the lot of the ordinary producer. Indeed, leadership is of such great importance, its quality so crucial to the success of social coordination, that a confusion tends to arise as to whether the efficiency and consequent surplus of production (above bare necessities of survival) are due to the social coordination *or* to the leadership which induces and directs it. Strategic position in the social structure has generally enabled leadership to decide this issue in its own favor, and to award itself ever increasing shares of the community's wealth. An economy may thus arise in which the productive population is kept at or near the subsistence level in a system of serfdom or slavery. Despite the political submersion, this was an economic gain at the dawn of history—a floor not a ceiling—when famine constantly threatened other nomadic groups in the surrounding wilderness. The value of adherence to such a community at any social level is one of the meanings of the scriptural account of Joseph in Egypt. The imposing monumentality of the tombs and temples of the Nile Valley, accomplished despite the availability only of the simplest forms of mechanical equipment, proclaim the complete submission of the productive population to the absolute dominion of a very small group.

Since it is largely surplus wealth that is dedicated to cultural production, choices determining the character of its forms will be made by— hence will express—those who control the expenditure of such funds. A limited amount of wealth and therefore some scope of independent cultural expression will fall to intermediate groups, who may emulate the taste and expression of the rulers, or possibly form a distinct "popular" culture of their own, as in the development of the modern theater during the seventeenth century. Even with the most meager resources a spirited people will develop some form of "folk art." Among the various forms of expression created at any one time for different social levels, greater or less homogeneity will obtain according to the character of the relations between the groups, and this is the limit to the reality of any such thing as an absolute *zeitgeist*. But in respect to monumental art, the endowment of considerable wealth is a necessary factor, whether from political, economic, religious or other sources, and therefore the most substantial cultural expressions will correspond predominantly to the concerns of community leaders who make the funds available, however widely and thoroughly they may be accepted by the rest of the population.

The notion of a mysteriously pervasive "spirit of the age," dictating arbitrary similarities of cultural expression in widely separated areas, must be unmasked as nothing more than a quite natural homogeneity of style in the art of people living the *same kind of life* regardless of locality. At one time theories of style in art gave inordinate importance to the place of origin, reflecting the pattern whereby each town or province had its own kind of cheese, soup or special shape of bread loaf. Some museums still label old masters simply "Dutch School," "English School," "Italian School," as though there were any such thing. These baseless implications of geographical distinction made similarities of style in different areas appear especially mysterious and remarkable when first noted, thus lending undue weight to the concept of the *zeitgeist*.

Similarities of linear quality in fifteenth-century style both of Flanders and Florence, for example, do not indicate a global ferment, radiation or circumambience that may be expected to influence expression similarly in India, Melanesia or North America. Those two communities were both leaders in a related form of commercial growth from which their citizens developed parallel views, interests and ways of life, and to this extent their cultural expression tended toward stylistic similarities.

A common objection to the proposal that style is determined by general thoughts and practices of a community or any section of it, arises from a fallacious interpretation that an artist "expresses *himself.*" The processes of creation are of course subjective in essence, regardless of any degree of conventionality that might be required of the artist from time to time; but even in the most subjective and individualistic periods, the artist must function as a member of some social group. From earliest infancy, basic techniques such as walking and talking are acquired by sheer imitation. Values, objectives, acceptable procedures are socially determined at least in essence. No one can survive as an artist, or at any rate genuinely participate in the cultural expression of the age, unless his work is successful in winning some response from persons capable of rendering adequate economic support. Today there are thousands of people in every art who function on a part-time basis and present the illusion of economic independence for their creative effort, but only those who outgrow this limited professional application can deeply affect the evolution of style.

In a market economy based on private ownership, costly works of art are purchased by wealthy patrons whose "taste" or cultural attitudes therefore exercise a decisive influence at least on the more luxurious forms of expression in their particular communities. At some stages of leadership's development its taste will coincide broadly with other interests in the community. At others, aristocratic forms will arise that vary sharply from popular ideals, like the court painting of the eighteenth century in France (Plate 37b).

The ethnic and technological factors which have been found above to influence style toward one or the other of the polar categories, represent cultural reactions to the struggle of the group with natural environment, or of the artist with technical problems of artistic creation. Socioeconomic influences are brought to bear on the development of style in art through the struggle of individuals or groups within the community to establish more effective social organization or to gain control of its leadership. Whatever force is involved, therefore, is not directed against the community as a whole, and basic cultural continuity is maintained, so that stylistic changes present a gradual, evolutionary appearance even in the establishment of a new order.

Changes in control due to force alone are characteristic mainly of very early stages of human history. In recent times, the rise of more successful methods of production and community organization has been an important reason for social reorganization with its changes in leadership, and consequently new channels for distribution of wealth. Change of this kind, involving force only as far as it is used by and against the few who feel deprived rather than benefited by the new order, has a much more profound effect on the way of life of the entire population than a mere change of personal leadership or dynasty, as when a pretender assassinated the legitimate heir or a palace mayor ousted a weakened imperial line. It is generally backed by fervent popular support, and brings about a noticeable change in cultural forms to express the ideals and enthusiasms inspired by new hopes of improving the common lot.

The Medici established their power in Florence with the aid of one of the first organizations of industrial workers, the "Ciompi" of the wool carders' trade, and their rule for several generations made Florence into one of the greatest cities of Europe. The common action of the "embattled farmers" in New England opened the way for the North American continent to develop into a great industrial community, instead of remaining an exploited agricultural appendage of British imperial economy. Though an element of force was involved in each case, the change in the order of things was actually made possible by the promise of a better life, which enlisted widespread popular support. The longevity of such general enthusiasm for a new order depends on the length of time the new leadership continues to identify its own power with the growth and well-being of the community. Dynastic succession, however, such as existed previous to the market economy, and which overlapped the early stages of the modern era for many centuries, tends to promote a gradual sense of distinction between the interests of the community and its leaders, the governing and the governed. The elite become interested rather in enjoying the luxuries they can command and in solidifying their power in absolute form. This involves exploitation and repression, and places them in a position essentially antagonistic to those they rule.

*Relation of Style to the Evolution of the Community.* A practical approach to the problems of social adjustment, resulting in analytical styles of cultural expression, will naturally characterize the procedures of those who are rising to power. In order to work out a new order they must of necessity be creative, devising and formulating new means of production and control. Alertness and ingenuity are needed to overcome obstacles raised by the powers they must displace, and to accumulate whatever sort of capital investment must be made. Gradual success, growing wealth will engender a certain self-reliance in the members of a rising social movement, a sense of personal adequacy to cope with the problems that arise, rather than a feeling of need for despotic power to eliminate them. New leaders will idealize order in terms similar to primitive analytical thought, for they must function on the basis of faith in clear, reliable and manageable patterns of what is real and to their purpose. Whereas the natural cosmos dominated the concern of primitive man, however, the culturally significant environment since the beginning of history has been the current social structure.

The clarified analytical forms of fifteenth-century Florentine art, in addition to the technological factors involved, express this practical outlook in the rising merchant leaders of the new city-state. Such an intensely "becoming" group eventually "becomes." Their superior techniques and abilities enrich the community and enlist its loyal support. Complete supremacy achieved, the new leaders need strive simply to maintain it, which becomes increasingly easy up to the point of a new fundamental challenge. A victorious leadership tends toward absolutism by appropriating the wealth of defeated forces, suppressing opposition and institutionalizing its control of all phases of community life. This includes the tendency of the dominant forces, or one dominant force within what might have begun as a relatively broad social movement, to assume and intensify complete control. It also includes a tendency toward increased formulation and conventionality in cultural expression, encouraged or dictated from above. The Medici first derived power from a political machine created to serve the needs of the new commercial interests through relatively democratic channels; but they finally assumed a hereditary title by force. The change in their attitude toward the community is signalized by the constantly increasing emphasis on the academic classicism of the Renaissance, which they promoted by supporting scholars, building libraries and collecting antiquities. Such esoteric concerns could have no vital meaning for more than an elite few hundred of the thousands who had been proudly dedicated to the practical activities that had first made the name of Florence great.

There is unmistakable significance in the difference between the subject of the *School of Athens* (Plate 26) which Raphael used in the Vatican in the sixteenth century, glorifying Aristotle and Plato as representative of classical ideology, and that of the *Banquet of Anthony and Cleopatra* (Plate 6) with which Tiepolo decorated the Palazzo Labia about two centuries later. The shift to political heroes of antiquity, among whom Alexander the Great is also a frequently used subject, expresses admiration for absolute rulers or their admiration of themselves.

Eventually, dynastic absolutism tends to discard all practical and moral responsibility. As concentration of wealth reaches imperial magnitude, only a small part is required to relieve the hereditary rulers from the burdens of management and control by retaining practical personnel at a hire sufficiently generous to give them a dedicated interest in the continuity of the *status quo*.

Style in the arts then becomes the expression of patrons and arbiters completely lacking any practical experience or concern. Even their personal needs may be administered to in a ridiculous degree by body servants. Such an aristocracy or plutocracy takes for granted that its complete and often arbitrary control of the lives of others is of sacred or divine origin, for succeeding generations lose sight of the constructive and responsible program that originally established the family's rule. Subconsciously mystified indeed by the absolute powers granted them without any practical demonstration of merit, they are impelled toward a sensational philosophy of accepting things as they are without any probing analysis. Detailed knowledge of processes whereby the life of the community is maintained becomes boring if not indeed fearsome to them. Their unaccountably eminent way of life, removed from the reassuring practicalities of production, cradled in luxury and maintained by centralized autocracy, is well expressed by the fluid, sensuous, contrived novelty of sensational style.

There are also positive factors tending toward sensational expression in the advanced stages of a given socioeconomic development. Later generations, reared in an atmosphere of gentility, will be familiar with the basic cultural formulations already established. Their sophistication forms a basis for freer, more intuitive developments and combinations in the arts, embodying liberalization and sensuous enrichment of first principles as these come to be taken for granted. Style then shows an increasingly complex and subtle intensification of familiar cultural forms. As the artist becomes capable, through creative experience, of more skillfully elaborated production, so the patron also becomes more capable of encompassing an increasingly complex constellation of aesthetic values. It is in this context that the great art of a so-called "Golden Age" is likely to occur, in which sensuous sophistication enriches familiar basic forms, instead of supplanting or distorting them.

Development of aesthetic effects and novelty in more complex sensational styles by later generations appeals predominantly to those leading members of society who can afford relatively luxurious surroundings and sufficient leisure in which to develop an understanding of progressively more involved and esoteric modes of expression. The vast productive population finds no expressive fulfillment in compounded subtlety carried to extremes, not only because a style completely concerned with sensation is antagonistic to practical expression, which must continue to be the popular cultural need, but also because they have neither the leisure nor the background of luxurious contact in which to develop an understanding of complex and esoteric subtlety.

Inaccessibility of complex styles to "uncultivated" minds, (uncultivated only in an ultimate sense not at all derogatory of their true character or intellect) becomes a positive value for the ruling group, as an apparent indication of their own superiority, a sort of cultural badge of justification for "divine right," and a means of overawing the deprived productive sections of the population. To this end the more obscure aspects of style are exaggerated, new distortions and unclarifications invented (such as extreme proportions, violent perspective, bizarre patterns of light and shade;) and unfamiliar subject matter is used, from the increasingly recondite mythology of the late Renaissance to the risqué, the romantic and the completely obscure.

Previous to the nineteenth century the luxurious complexity of the baroque and rococo styles at the French court (Plate 37b) had been sufficient to impress the rivaling nobility or "*épater les bourgeois*," but thereafter, bombastic assertions of power were no longer taken seriously by the rising entrepreneurs. The broad advances in economic and cultural democracy during the nineteenth and twentieth centuries have challenged any self-designated elite much more sharply than has ever been done before, and have engendered in the so-called "connoisseur" a capricious delight in resorting to cultural blind alleys, sleight-of-hand and critical double talk to confuse the sincere interest of the much larger public, whose practical burden in an economy of plenty no longer completely precludes informed cultural interests. In this situation, sensationalism no longer means simply attention to summary aesthetic aspects or intensifications of reality, but rather a positive rejection of reality in favor of various exploitations of sensation itself (previously referred to as "postillusionistic sensationalism," p. 37).

With all objective reference eliminated or so deeply submerged as to be recognized only with considerable guidance, there is no means of contact with art for a large number of otherwise cultured individuals among the numerous skilled, managerial, professional and intellectual personnel of modern industrial society. It would seem that it might therefore be rewarding for these practical-minded groups and the artists who would prefer to serve them, to turn their backs on the smart and glittering sophistication of much currently acclaimed art and establish an independent, more analytical expression closer to their own genuine interests. Brilliant accomplishments along these lines have already been made outside the plastic arts in such fields as documentary literature and films, and in some areas of the drama. Similarly during the seventeenth and eighteenth centuries the bourgeoisie in Europe had a highly accomplished expression of their own in the plastic arts entirely distinct from the brilliant court styles. The truly astounding production of Rembrandt and the "little" Dutch masters may be considered its crowning glory (Plate 39), but it flourished elsewhere as in the work of the so-called "*bambocianti*" of Italy, and the Le Nain-de Latour-Chardin tradition in France (Plate 37a).

During the nineteenth century, likewise, America produced a strong, independent realistic expression in the plastic arts, exemplified by the work of such figures as Charles Willson Peale, who spanned the Revolutionary period, Bingham (Plate 25a) and Mount early in the nineteenth century, Homer and Eakins at the end, and there was considerable vitality in landscape painting generally. Constant competition to this development of a genuine native expression came from fashionable attempts to emulate European art, which gained ascendancy in the "Hegira" of the late nineteenth century, when the figure of J. A. McN. Whistler (Plate 25b) was elevated to a position of commanding importance. American cultural independence in the plastic arts was virtually submerged by this influence toward the end of World War II.

Thus it appears that whereas analytical and sensational attitudes seemed to have a sequential relation early in the development of European culture, the stages they represented are no longer as distinct as they once were. Cultural interests of both sorts may be supported simultaneously according to their expression of different social roles, like the concurrent aristocratic and bourgeois styles that flourished from the late Gothic period in Europe, and the competing pioneer and "nabob" interests in America. There was a practical quality about one extreme, an artificiality about the other, that may well be said to express in modern society the simultaneous roles of "producer" and "consumer," which will be discussed at greater length  after considerations of certain complications of the evolutionary pattern that are involved.

# 4

## Complications
## of the Evolutionary Process

CLEARLY THE MOST CURSORY VIEW OF CULTURAL HISTORY INDICATES THAT
the style of a work of art, the character of its forms, is affected by the
conditions under which the artist and his patrons live. In broadest outline, a society evolves from a stage in which human power and intelligence
achieve new successes, to one in which the descendants of inventive
founders relax in an atmosphere of self-satisfaction and nonchalance.
These opposite roles, which may variously be identified with similar
alternatives of creation and control, humanism and mysticism, social
orientation and individualism, and the roles of producer and consumer
especially after about 1800, may be said to be "expressed" respectively
by analytical and sensational form because they give rise to concepts and
practices reflected by these styles in art.

The process of evolution from one pole to another is not automatic
nor uniform, nor does each "cycle" start from exactly the same place;
and a relation to specific historical factors is always apparent. "Planimetric" applied to Greek relief sculpture means no reference to deep

101

space whatsoever, complete preservation of the surface to which it is applied. In painting or pictorial relief of the fifteenth century, however, it means construction of deep space, but always with regard for the plane; and some degree of spatial illusionism characterizes styles of both categories from this point on. Space in a painting by the Flemish painter Breughel (Plate 5b) is far more recessional than in a painting by Leonardo da Vinci (Plate 5a), who occupies a comparable stage in the development of Italian art, but Leonardo's chiaroscuro is considerably more optic than the almost unshaded figures of the Flemish master. Yet for all the recessional quality of Breughel's paintings, his compositions are firmly closed, and certainly later styles of art produce space that is more recessional than that of Breughel in character if not in distance covered, and description of form that is far more optic than Leonardo's.

The polar categories should not be considered in any sense as classifications for works of art or even for complete styles. They are rather a pattern of observation for analyzing style, as temperature, humidity, air pressure and wind velocity are observations for analyzing weather and climate. In these terms hot or cold weather, wet or dry, calm or windy, may be described with objective scientific accuracy for comparison of one season with another, one area with another, and so on. Unfortunately the polar categories have no simple index of quantity that can be stated in numerical degrees, pounds per square inch or miles per hour. Critical judgments must be made subjectively by personal agents whose preparation and impartiality can only be relatively perfect, and their conclusions should be subject to constant review by anyone who seeks to interpret expression in the arts for himself.

Although it is true that all of the characteristics of each of the polar categories *tend* to appear in mutually exclusive association, because any given society seems to be motivated predominantly by one attitude or another, there are specific situations in which this is not quite true. Not only are changes of style accomplished in a gradual evolution resulting in intermediary stages of complex character, but also cultural motivations of any given society tend to become increasingly complex as the historical continuity of its tradition lengthens. Except for the black page of Europe's early colonial expansion, no cataclysmic submergence has quite cut off any culture since the beginning of recorded history, as famine or drought must have taken whole tribal societies repeatedly in the earlier, prehistoric times, or as human violence frequently destroyed an entire culture with its social organization in the great struggles that led to the first major coordination of peoples. Thus prehistoric Aegaean culture was wiped out by the invading Dorians, although they adopted some elements; but the resulting Greek expression has remained a constant example ever since.

Because of such cultural comminglings, and other complexities of influence in the arts, no style can simply be assigned a position on a linear scale between the two poles. A graph in which ordinate and abscissa might indicate the dual motivation of a given style in terms of geoclimatic factors on one, and socioeconomic or evolutionary position on the other would be better; but the observation that influences carry over from one "cycle" to another, narrowing the gap, would require a three-dimensional graph, tending to complicate the explanation beyond the point of serviceability. Some value might be found in a conical graph, with the complete opposition of the basic categories represented by opposite sides of the circle at the lowest level, and the narrowing diameter of each ascending spiral representing their tendency to draw closer together with time. This would correspond to the eventual combination of opposites already noted (p. 32) in the philosophy of science, where it is now recognized that neither logical speculation nor exhaustive natural observation alone are sufficient, but that practical knowledge must be based on an adequate balance of induction and deduction.

Until careful study of such possibilities can be made, however, it must suffice simply to observe certain characteristic situations in which stylistic motivation is obviously complex. There are at least four typical situations, two following directly from the evolutionary process, namely: (1) *transitions of growth,* in which the style must pass through a middle ground partaking somewhat of both extremities; and (2) *transitions of change,* in which vestiges of previous sophistication are inevitably involved in the formulation of a new expression, however practical. Two others are (3) provincialism, and (4) eclecticism, and the purpose of the present section is to consider all four in turn.

TRANSITIONS OF GROWTH: THE GOLDEN AGE

The enveloping spatial volume of Raphael's *School of Athens* (Plate 26), with the principal figures of Aristotle and Plato composed almost at the limit of its depth, may be said to be recessional by comparison with space in earlier fifteenth-century compositions where the principal figures are placed strictly at the picture plane as though posed at the footlights before a painted theatrical backdrop of the landscape. Nevertheless Raphael's space is obviously constructed of planes parallel to the picture plane, and is consequently planimetric by comparison with the style of Tintoretto (Plate 12b). It might be said that Raphael's composition is planimetric in spatial structure and recessional in the distribution of figures. This quality of seeming to combine opposite polar characteristics results quite naturally from the fact that evolution between the poles is a gradient, not a jump.

Works of this sort coincide with a relatively distinct period in the evolution of a culture, often referred to as a "Golden Age," like the Periclean age of Greece, or the Italian high Renaissance, the particular quality of which they clearly express. In view of the fact that the styles of such periods represent an evolutionary midpoint at which some contact with both poles is felt, they might be called "transitions of growth." These styles do not come about, however, as a mere evolutionary accident, but express a definite stage in socioeconomic evolution, reflecting a precise personality which emerges in these times.

Before the period of modern finance, huge fortunes could not be amassed in a single generation. A series of two, three or perhaps more generations of creative, practical persons was required to develop power to a point where security, luxury and leisure would induce a completely sensational culture. Individuals whose role is the development of inherited power are reared against a background of increasing comfort, luxury and sophistication. As patrons of art, such people would have a quite developed understanding of the nature of cultural expression, taste regarding established formulations in art, some feeling for luxury and social refinement, combined with an essentially analytical attitude toward environment related to their necessarily practical approach in the conduct of affairs.

The Medici family is an outstanding example. The Florentine court at which Lorenzo the Magnificent (1449–1492) was raised, had already achieved considerable elegance and intellectual brilliance in the reign of his grandfather, Cosimo. In his youth he had access to the companionship of the leading artists, poets and philosophers of his day. These were no sycophants at the feet of power, but genuine pioneering talents, assiduously drawn into the aristocratic circle for their intelligence and ability, without consideration of birth or courtliness, generally so much more important in later stages. The Medici are said, for example, to have constructed the monastery of St. Mark's for the Dominican group at Fiesole, of which Fra Angelico was a member, within the city limits in order to make him a Florentine.

Lorenzo himself wrote such excellent verse in the popular Italian tongue (and in Latin too, which he gave up as an obstacle to local cultural progress) that he is credited with being a potent force in saving its artistic future from submergence in the flood of academic literature in Greek and Latin that was being translated and composed by members of his own court. But his political life was far from a sinecure. As a youth he faced death at the hands of the Pazzi conspirators, who killed his brother in an attack on the pair during High Mass. Fighting them off, he escaped and proceeded ruthlessly to stamp out the entire cabal. He intrigued endlessly, managed to alter the republican system of Florence to ensure his own political power, furthered the commercial fortunes of Florence and ruled as a personal dictator.

Lorenzo's son Giovanni (1475–1521) as Pope Leo X, though power came to him more easily, had an active and complex career highlighted by the struggle against the heresies of Martin Luther, campaigns against Selim I in the Levant, maintenance of wide papal conquests in Italy, and control of foreign military and political influence within his domains. At the same time he was a patron of learning and made Rome the center of European culture. It is not surprising that Raphael (1483–1520) was among the artists whom he patronized, and that the greatest art of all time may be found in such periods where the strength of analytical form and structure is graced and enlivened with incipient sensational qualities.

Michelangelo (Plate 14a) and Titian (Plate 24), longer-lived contemporaries of Raphael, with him and a host of competent lesser figures, gave the plastic arts in sixteenth-century Italy a Golden Age of magnificent proportions. In Michelangelo's painting and sculpture, as well as in some of his architectural designs, nearly all the characteristics of the succeeding Baroque are present, yet in contrast with any seventeenth-century work they have a distinct clarity and tactile force no longer present in the later style. Such amalgamation of analytical and sensational values indicates an important possibility of guiding human culture, discussed later in relation to the expression of producer and consumer.

TRANSITIONS OF CHANGE: RECOMMENCEMENT

Combinations of seemingly contradictory stylistic characteristics are to be found also in periods when a new section of society is rising to power within a developed culture. This type of combination represents the persistence of old forms in a period when a new power is "recommencing" the cultural "cycle." Usage, familiarity or "taste" account for the continuation of these otherwise extraneous elements. Despite the fact that they do not convey the necessary practicality of the new leaders, the traditional aspects may legitimately express their admiration for a spiritual culture symbolizing to them the coveted wealth and social power. Success soon liquidates this early reverence, however, and the extraneous survivals disappear.

Even the most cataclysmic of political events rarely if ever fully destroys established cultural forms. In the case of a developed community extending its power over weaker neighbors, the culture of the conquering group would obviously be superimposed on, if not substituted for, any indigenous development of whatever stage. An energetic community might be moved, on the other hand, by an inferior standard of living to improve its lot through the conquest of a more developed, wealthier and perhaps decadent neighbor. Should it succeed, the superior aesthetic forms and objects, as well as the means of producing them, would constitute an important phase of the spoils of victory. In either event, the submerged culture almost invariably affects the succeeding forms in a degree inversely proportionate to the relative stage of development the conquering group has attained.

Greek sculpture by the boatload accompanied governors and generals home to Rome, and many of the craftsmen in Rome were Greek slaves or freedmen. Egyptian culture survived many conquests by barbarian neighbors. The Minoans, Mycenaeans and Etruscans, although they were wiped out by their relatively barbarian conquerors, probably because of the violence of their resistance, nevertheless left substantial traces among the forms of the succeeding Greek and Roman cultures. Classical art and thought exerted an extremely important influence on subsequent societies, surviving the impact of eastern nomadic tribes, and reappearing in countless forms, especially after the Middle Ages.

Since the beginning of recorded history, the productive organization and personnel of a given community have constituted an asset which political overlords with any judgment have been anxious to maintain. Thus the continuity of craftsmanship and other basic productive activities has remained virtually unbroken through seething changes of ideology and control in the Western world for about three thousand years. To a remarkable degree, the great battles of history were comparatively small and highly localized affairs, of considerable strategic importance but doing a minimum of violence to the social fabric as a whole, and wars at one time were suspended seasonally for attention to agricultural production. The rise of the market economy in Europe facilitated changes of power by constantly increasing fluidity of material assets and the credit structure. Even political conquest came to be based largely on consolidations of commercial control, to which any violence in the seizure of the reins of government was only secondary.

Despite occasional periods of iconoclasm, the evolutionary type of change since the rise of the market has tended to preserve the cultural forms and products of the past, and they have remained to a great extent accessible to succeeding generations. Thus a period representing a transition from one style to another, which might be referred to as a "transition of change," is characterized by some oddly assorted qualities which apparently contradict the basic applicability of either stylistic category. At such times, isolated sensational characteristics appear in an otherwise generally analytical style, for the reason that the declining culture will of course have achieved a relatively sensational stage, but the new order begins again with analytical practices and cultural expression.

Poussin (Plate 27a), for example, represents the beginning of a new stylistic cycle expressing a major social adjustment in France as a modern nation emerged there in the seventeenth century, and his compositions are seen to be quite discrete and planimetric; but he is certainly far less linear, more optic for his tonal description of form, especially in landscape painting, than any fifteenth-century Florentine. Hogarth is a highly analytical personality, speculating abstractly about theories of ideal beauty and analyzing social morality in topical compositions and series (Plate 27b). Stylistically his works are likewise analytical, as in the closed quality of his proscenium-like compositions, clarification of detail, and multiple emphasis on many different characters. Yet in contrast with most Italian Renaissance painting his treatment of form and materials is distinctly optic.

Thus transitional periods, both transitions of change as well as transitions of growth, demonstrate again that a given work or style is not to be assigned exclusively to one category or the other. It is rather to be described in terms of the individual polar characteristics that appear in it, which are at these points most likely to be somewhat qualified by or associated with some of their categorical opposites. The combinations seem to be most harmonious in a Golden Age, more contradictory and confused in a new social order, but in either case there is a valid correspondence with the expressive functions of the particular style.

## PROVINCIALISM

Provincial art often presents a situation similar to transitions of change, in that an essentially analytical attitude is superimposed upon an admired or inherited model that is sensational in style. This is due to the attempt of untrained and imperfectly trained artists to reconstruct the culture of a leading metropolitan center in a less developed or completely frontier situation. Lacking the highly evolved skills of sensational virtuosity (for the best-trained craftsmen survive adequately and remain in the more comfortable and important parent center), and with insufficient opportunity to develop an understanding of the type of form they are trying to create, provincial artists and craftsmen are forced to proceed tentatively, with detailed application not conducive to sensational fluency of style. As in the case of archaic artists struggling with expressive ideals beyond their immediate technological grasp, they must figure out their procedures from step to step. Thus personal and environmental limitations, bringing out the artist's practical ingenuity, force them to adopt an analytical procedure; but instead of applying it directly to the objective world, which would involve no contradiction, they try thus to recreate an inherited sensational style no longer pertinent to the surrounding mode of life.

The culture of a colonizing homeland is characteristically that of a relatively complex stage, because colonies result from the economic advantage of projecting surplus wealth or managerial resources into undeveloped regions. Provincial settlers, however, involved in the tremendously practical task of establishing production and winning subsistence from the wilderness, must adopt a resourcefully analytical approach in their daily lives almost as in a completely new society. The difference lies in the fact that they will remember and also import clothing, furniture and other goods, including some works of art, corresponding in style to the sensational stage of the homeland culture. Thus the artists are faced with models in a sensationally complex style beyond their professional skill, and foreign, if not to their conscious ideals, at least to the subconscious tutelage of the life around them.

Craftsmen who bring with them training in techniques of the parent culture do not encounter conditions conducive to their complete realization. There is no time for the more delicate refinements and complex structures, certain materials and tools are not available, trained assistance cannot be had. But also the sense of values is profoundly changed, for the pioneer must be a practical person. Only in centers of vice-regal contact can there be any purpose in seeking to distinguish oneself by means of artificialities imitated from metropolitan or homeland manners and dress. The interdependence of men in a new contact with nature creates either a special humanism of the frontier or an antisocial feeling of isolation and outlawry, neither of which has any interest in elaborately formalized social intercourse.

Contradictions between the necessarily analytical approach and the merely reminiscent sensational model tend to produce that spotty, dry, wooden appearance that commonly identifies provincial work (Plate 28). Parenthetically it might be added that a very similar contradiction in aims and appearance arises in the work of naïve, "modern primitive" artists or "Sunday painters" (Plate 29b). In terms of the polar categories, the characteristics of these styles include: (1) A crispness of detail due to analytical clarification of forms obviously intended in the parent style to convey optic fusion, like sharp, mechanical highlights on clothing, or overprecise repetition of illusionistic conventions for representing foliage. (2) Clarification and equal emphasis of parts despite the use of compositional devices characteristic of sensational fusion and centrality, such as a pyramidal arrangement of figures that are too independently developed to fuse structurally for the intended effect. (3) Depth in composition (either of a painting, a piece of carved decoration, or an architectural facade) will be reduced to an analytical insistence on plane; as for example, a graceful *contrapposto* may be flattened into a grotesquely sharp reversal of direction from one section of the body to another; salient pilasters of a recessional façade in the Baroque manner are reduced to mere lines; or a figure made small to suggest distance, pops up to the picture plane (for the sharpness of its drawing) like an image pasted on a plate-glass window.

Even in the work of John Singleton Copley, possibly colonial America's finest painter, some of these qualities appear. In his portrait of *The*

*Copley Family* (Plate 28b) it can be seen without any disparagement of the forceful realization of the forms presented, that their analytical, tactile reality is contradicted somewhat by the attempt at optic tonality. This contributes also to the spatial contradiction between the intended recession and the planimetric contact of all the forms with the picture plane. Thus the head of the artist seems to be suspended uncomfortably in mid-air over that of his stepfather, and there can be no nearer volume of space for the little girl in the center despite the fact that she overlaps the adjacent figures. The glimpse of landscape also pushes forward, more like a painted backdrop than a genuine depth.

In the work of many of the less accomplished or less trained colonial artists, as well as in that of the later "primitives" like Henri Rousseau (Plate 29b), and many lesser figures here and abroad, the underlying analytical qualities achieve a self-justifying harmony totally independent of any stylistic model. This appears strikingly for example in the more "naïve" portraits of American colonial "limners" and others of the early nineteenth century, which often achieve great tactile force, pleasing rhythm of composition and analytical detail, as well as a rich and graceful flow of uninterrupted outline (Plate 28a). Typical stylistic irrelevancies are an oddly unrealized conventionalization of highlights especially on clothing, and occasional failures of perspective.

If a complete economic development occurs in the colony, making it independent of the mother country, an independent cultural expression arises in due course. Faesolium and Lutetia were provincial seats of the Roman Empire, but as they subsequently grew into the capitals of Tuscany and France, they created leading expressions of European culture. An understanding of American art is not possible without reference to this principle. Independent qualities of American culture are obscured, perhaps because of the rapidity with which political and economic independence developed in the Western Hemisphere, by the fact that highly skilled native artists and craftsmen continue to be dependent on an unquestionably higher degree of sophistication found in European models, without reference to the fact that the persisting dynamic character of the social order in America, and the practical influence still felt from recent pioneering experience, limit the value of sophistication in cultural expression for the American public.

To be sure there is a small circle whose cultural background is virtually transatlantic, as there has always been in America since the days of vice-regal governors and royal charters, as well as a considerable fringe who feel impelled to emulate their tastes and manners as a means of demonstrating their admiration for the mighty. This interest has admirably succeeded in supporting refinements of the highest order in American life, at least one important opera company, several internationally noted symphony orchestras and fine museums, some genuine *haute couture,* as well as *cuisine* and *bel servizio* in the leading hotels and restaurants of an excellence such that no European of whatever station need look forward to an American sojourn as the type of ordeal he would have anticipated one or two hundred years ago. Such accomplishment is hardly the result of independent evolution, but rather of assiduous imitation, which is a legitimate short cut in the minor arts and "creature comforts," where craftsmanship alone and not expression is involved. Unfortunately there are areas, especially among the plastic arts, where independent expression of important cultural attitudes is hindered by this peculiar type of nabobism that persists despite the international economic and political power of the United States.

The unique experience of the people on the North American continent in carving a comfortable existence out of a wilderness, in integrating the broadest forms of political democracy and the largest free trade area that have existed in the modern world, and in giving a clear track to the development of mass industry, has created a philosophy, personal interests, ways of doing business and of getting along with people, that are clearly distinct in sum from those of any other time or place. Perhaps it is too soon to look for a complete expression of this independence in monumental art. Considerable strides were made in American painting of the nineteenth century (Plate 25a). It remains to be seen whether the submergence of interest in artists like Charles Willson Peale, George Caleb Bingham, W. S. Mount and the better known figures of Eakins and Homer, and the rupture of tradition which it represents, is a temporary eddy; and if not, what it augurs for the future of the plastic arts in America.

### ECLECTICISM

Much has been written to argue the virtues of one eclectic model or another in the plastic arts during the past few centuries. The battle of the Poussinistes versus the Rubenistes in France, of the admirers of Raphael versus the adherents of Michelangelo more or less throughout Europe, and the "battle of the styles" when the virtues of the Gothic were advanced against those of the classic in England, have produced much sound and fury, signifying mainly a profound confusion regarding the role of art in human society. The very impulse to cast cultural expression in a form imitated from a distant land or age seems to contradict the principles of a profound expressive relation between art and life. However, there have been times, for reasons similar to those that cause stylistic confusion in a provincial situation, when artists have been instructed by their patrons to abandon contemporary practice and model their production on that of some other society. The original revival of classical form in the Italian Renaissance had ample justification, as a citation of ancient and revered authority for its humanistic revolt against ecclesiastical obscurantism, but it set a precedent that has been followed in other circumstances to much less fitting purpose, and has resulted in various cultural confusions. It is all very well to wave with friendly enthusiasm the flag of an allied nation, but there must be profound reasons for a complete shift of allegiance away from one's native land.

To be sure, tradition is a legitimate and necessary base for any advancement of the arts, which must in some degree refer to all previous and contemporary formulations with which it is in contact. Only by tradition may culture avoid constant return to primitive inadequacies; only by repeated overlays of technical experience can art achieve the tremendous richness of formal and expressive complexity found in the most admired styles. Eclectic imitation weakens the expressive validity of a style chiefly when contact with the antecedent model is insufficiently intimate. When references to the past take the form of abstract, archaeological counterfeit, and when the choice is motivated by pretentious superficial whims rather than appropriate plastic impulses, eclecticism has a false and confusing ring. The plight of W. S. Gilbert's hapless Bunthorne, as he mournfully confessed, came about because "In short, my medievalism's affectation, Born of morbid love of admiration."

In terms of the polar categories, eclecticism is one of those forces which may produce an otherwise unaccountable combination of contradictory qualities of form, or a failure of the form to correspond to its appropriate expressive role. However, whereas provincialism, which causes a similar confusion, invariably results from injection of extraneous sensational qualities into a properly analytical style, eclecticism frequently brings about the opposite. Academic reference, during the last century or two, to models from classical antiquity has been a great source of stylistic confusion. Attempting to use canonical formulations of the classic type, and apparently favoring tactile form, the official style of the École des Beaux Arts in France, for example, has appeared to employ an analytical approach throughout a period in which sensational expression seemed to be more pertinent in view of various other social factors, as well as by the obvious vitality and critical success of a sensational trend in art from Delacroix (Plate 38b) to the present. The Pre-Raphaelite Brotherhood in England (Plate 29a) and similar movements elsewhere, despite strenuous efforts to achieve the honest lack of sophistication that to them was expressed by the linear style of Italian *quattrocento* art, show in their paintings obvious delicacies of illumination and surface quality, fusion of form and composition, and spatial unity clearly indicating their nineteenth-century origin. Art which involves such contradictions between spirit and style, however, is rarely marked by obvious disharmony such as appears in provincial art, but rather by the utmost virtuosity as in the paintings of Bouguereau, or for that matter most of the forgotten work exhibited in the salons of Europe throughout the nineteenth century.

Superficial eclecticism arises in large part from a prevalent concept that culture and art serve as a mask for the practical actualities of life. Impressed by the glitter of court functions, many merchants and craftsmen of the eighteenth and nineteenth centuries accepted the aristocratic estimate of their own manners and expression as uncouth, and strove as they became economically powerful and culturally self-conscious to imitate the presumably superior artificiality of their defeated rivals. It became their ambition as soon as possible to cultivate art and manners as a superficial gloss or shell intended to obscure the inferior and unsatisfactory aspects of their way of life, like a row of bushes to screen an unpleasant view, or that patriotism which is so often cited as "the last refuge of a scoundrel."

Unfortunately the consequence of this early bourgeois identification of art with artificiality and aristocracy, was that when successful practical personalities in the nineteenth and twentieth centuries felt no further awe of inherited social status and achieved the complete cultural self-respect rightfully due their personal accomplishments, they could see no further use for art! Conditioned to regard art as a pretentious assertion, they could not see how it could be used to assert the positive, genuine values in their lives. This is the basis for much perfectly sound "Philistinism" that has been so bitterly assailed during the past century or so, especially by artists.

Almost completely submerged is faith in the beauty of directly expressing a life which is conducted in as fitting and noble a manner as human beings individually and together can achieve. This is the true and indispensable function for art in a healthy society. To be sure, "expression" does not mean mere depiction of life exactly as it happens to be. It is legitimate to divert attention away *from* incompleteness and failure *toward* aims and successes. Such glorification of life is a prideful and positive course, socially useful for accomplishing realistic ideals rather than a negative and cringing emulation of the ways of the mighty.

A considerable variety of social maladjustments still support eclectic cultural expression as a mask or shell that may be donned complete, with little reference to the inhabitant shape. A ready-made culture suits people of immature responsibility, who can enjoy effortless leisure, freedom from necessary activity or obligation. Eclectic pretensions also frequently cast art in the role of shield or apologist for leadership entrenched beyond the limits of its social usefulness, or actively predatory and antisocial, like the personal elegance notoriously affected by racketeering gangsters; or the palaces, and collections of old masters owned by the so-called "robber barons" of the late nineteenth century. Academic dependence on classical models also provides a convenient mode of official generalization, a dignified way of taking a stand against sin and for everything noble without committing the management or the regime to any too precise or practical program.

The "shell concept" of culture serves also as a defensive camouflage in personal expression, necessitated by the increasingly destructive character of some forms of contemporary economic and social competition. In diplomacy, politics, business, the insincere cultivation of personal contacts for material advantage involves constant resort to dissembling and falsification. Even a perfectly honest man today would no more mention unorthodox political enthusiasms outside the most intimate circles of his acquaintance, than he would dash down the middle of a street under fire in modern warfare.

Certain forms of sentimental personal expression, like ostentatiously fondling a baby or patronizing an economic inferior, enable a person of no particular character apparently to assume appropriate virtues at will. Eclecticism likewise serves as a gesture toward the whole calendar of virtues accredited to all the societies of history. The classic columns of a bank protest the clear-sighted solidity and all-embracing power for which the Roman Empire is admired; or in a government building, the democratic social dedication of the citizenry of ancient Greece. Soaring Gothic vaults and spires proclaim the piety presumed to have inspired a medieval community's devotion to the kingdom of heaven, and the fine row of French chateaux in replica that once lined New York's Fifth Avenue asserted groundless pretensions to ancient and noble lineage by great commercial fortunes.

Still another factor in modern life favoring such artificial forms of cultural expression as eclecticism, is the ease with which power may change hands without general disturbance of society or damage to the productive organism. Great wealth is sometimes acquired so rapidly that there is no time for a new millionaire or group (railroad, banking, butter and egg, oil) of millionaires to develop a new expression particularly appropriate to their own conditions. Little enough time to find out what art and culture are all about. Better call in an interior decorator and a social secretary.

Preciosity and virtuosity become the marks of such a culture. The most subtle and sensuous of abstract forms and lush materials (or in an earlier day, the most highly skilled imitation of fashionably admired antecedents) are applied by the sophisticated professional practitioner to the environment of the new arrivals "in the money," who boast (or try to forget) their early days as a puddler, dishwasher, truck driver, bootlegger or just a growing boy "back on the farm." To be sure, it is not long before some of these late-come patrons of elegance, or at least their wives and children, master the glib sophistication thus provided, and even achieve genuine discrimination or "taste"; the vanity of others will be titillated by the ingenuity, strangeness and costly appearance of a fashionable setting, while still others will conform but inwardly prefer their old, overstuffed upholstery or "mission oak" furniture with topical prints on the wall. In any case, there is little or no deep emotional expression represented by the owner's response to the intrinsic quality of the forms in an arbitrarily fabricated stylishness.

Academically, eclecticism presents certain obvious possibilities for enrichment or reorientation of expression by revealing the wealth of previous invention as a challenge, like a pacer in a distance race. In the recent past, however, it has served mainly to aggravate a deep-seated confusion regarding the function of art, by providing, as it were, a strangely assorted platter of hors d'oeuvres for people who would much prefer a large hamburger. Museums present fine works from all ages and lands, some more spectacular, others less, in styles expressing the gamut of human attitudes. However, the value of such a perspective is lost if, instead of choosing from among the variety something to follow because it applies to their own way of life, the public lose themselves in gaping and bewildered wonderment, while their professional mentors devote themselves to useless polemics about which good is better, or protest the impossibility of guiding anyone into the mystery they so ecstatically cherish. In obscuring the spiritual nourishment and social hygiene of a cultural expression genuinely related to the positive aspects of any given society, eclecticism has most seriously eroded the foundations of latter-day cultural expression in the plastic arts.

## STYLISTIC PROBLEMS IN THE USE OF TRADITION

For a variety of reasons it is impossible to think of the polar categories as exclusive classifications of works or periods of art, or to see their evolutionary relation and the appearance of a cyclical repetition as a simple mechanical spin round and round the same old path; and all past suggestions of automatic character in the evolutionary tendencies of cultural development should be eliminated. Repetitions of the tactile to optic or classic to baroque sequence occur simply because certain conditions tend to grow naturally and therefore repeatedly out of others in the human process of building a community. The basic pattern shows clearly only in those periods of history when motivations are least complex, or over a span broad enough to submerge incidental deviations.

In latter-day culture the continuity seems less smooth than in the development of Greek art or the Italian Renaissance. Particular stylistic manifestations of certain periods in the history of art may seem to upset the basic pattern of growth from analysis to sensation, or the relation of these polar attitudes to early and late stages, to producer or consumer interests; but in each case there are special circumstances clearly motivating the divergence, to be discovered by sufficient examination and thought. An attempt has been made here only to generalize about conditions governing various types of evolutionary transition from one polar category to another, as well as in provincial situations and in periods when eclectic imitation seems to belie the expressive role of art.

Further study of the far from simple motivation of various phases of Neo-classicism is a broad field; and much might be worked out regarding the true social meaning of sixteenth-century Italian Mannerism as an eddy in the brisk current from the high Renaissance to the Baroque.

A careful evaluation is yet to be made of the revolutionary protestations that have accompanied the appearance of certain phases of the twentieth-century trend toward abstraction, as well as the apparently analytical qualities of line and plane in these otherwise highly aestheticized, abstract and nonobjective styles.

A certain obvious continuity in cultural development, indicated by the basic evolutionary pattern of the polar categories, may give to the history of art the semblance of a stream rising in the hills and flowing to the sea, but it must not be thought that it falls only of its own weight, simply according to an invariable gravitational pull, for then the course of all rivers would be the same. The course of the stream is determined entirely by the terrain, which for the stream of art would be the shape of human society. The waters must conform to the banks that contain them, and move slowly or precipitously as the channel falls. So if the entire stream could be congealed and lifted from its geographical context as a picture can be removed from its historical context, it would be possible to read precisely the shape of the river bed. Wildly rushing waters would indicate or "express" the rugged, precipitous bed of the rapids, well upstream; slow, even movement would clearly imply the broad, gently falling bed of the river lower down the valley or crossing the broad plain near the end of its journey.

Narrow, fast and rough in the headwaters, slow, broad and easy near the sea is the pattern repeated in one river after another. But is this an intrinsic, inevitable quality of running water, or a condition imposed on it repeatedly by the constant logic of geology? Should the bed broaden momentarily at the base of a fall high in the hills, it would cause a quiet pool to form far above the level where slow movement is expected. Should a great boulder or fallen tree block the motion of the water, there would be an eddy in which the direction of movement will reverse that of the river itself.

Such is the relationship that the stream of cultural expression bears to the evolution of human society. Identification of the polar categories of form with an evolutionary sequence of stylistic development and basic tendencies of ethnic character is not intended as a revelation of arbitrary or esoteric conditions in the plastic arts, but rather as an exposition of a perfectly legible pattern of their illuminating correspondence with the development of human society. The following section will describe, in a broad way, how the chief phases in the history of Western culture appear under examination in these terms.

# 5

# Reading the Outlines of History in the Evolution of Style

THERE IS LITTLE GENERAL AGREEMENT ABOUT THE CULTURAL QUALITY OF past ages, but in this respect the art critics have been handicapped by the failure of historians to agree on, or even to be much concerned with, more than a string of accurately dated incidents, a limitation forced on them to some extent by the bugaboo of scientific "factualism" in the social sciences. Surely factual accuracy is a necessary base, and the time is well spent in truing it. Meanwhile, however, vague subjective guesses in the neglected area of social interpretation have led to various confusions. How "other-worldly" was a crafty Gothic merchant, how "humanistic" a swaggering high Renaissance duke? Many have been cited as the "father" of the modern age, from Dante and Giotto to J. J. Rousseau and J. L. David or Eugene Delacroix; but what, indeed, is the precise distinction of any span so designated?

Recent historical writing seems to be tending very promisingly away from the old molecular approach, in which any form of generalization was scorned and scholarship or authority was established by the accumulation of ever smaller, more esoteric and unmanageable detail. Perhaps

118

such an approach was necessary to correct unfounded, subjective, medieval types of generalization, as well as distortions wrought in the interests of nationalistic pride. In order to make history more "scientific," it was thought obvious that the methods of science must be followed, albeit the only recognized science was in the natural field. All of the social sciences have been afflicted at some stage or other by the same confusion or oversight regarding what *for them* are scientific criteria.

The natural sciences began to be successful when they discovered the means of *breaking down* their material into component elements, molecules, atoms, subatomic particles; into tissues, cells and cellular structure. But the social sciences must *start* with cells and atoms—there's one now, crossing the street, and three others are standing at the corner chatting. Some sixty million of them go to work every day in the United States alone, and a comparable number into the retail market. But the tissues and substances these cells and atoms form are not so easily seen. Even individual psychology can be understood only by relating the traits and actions of its subjects to the widest possible range of comparable manifestations. Whereas the crucial tool for the natural sciences might thus be said to be the *microscope,* which made possible the study of the *composition* of matter, the need in the social sciences is for a *macroscope* to discover what bodies people *compose.*

The word *body* is a clear key. The natural sciences study the human body *anatomically* as bone, muscles, nerves, veins, the cellular structure and chemical elements of its component materials, and so on. How *bodies of people* act is the concern of the social sciences, for the action of any single person may be completely idiosyncratic and practical knowledge must be more widely based; but what social body any particular person most significantly belongs to cannot readily be discerned. Does he push and rush that way because he is a New Yorker, an American, a hell-fearing Protestant, a Caucasian, a small businessman, an only son, an adolescent, a paranoid or a manic-depressive?

Obviously the instrument that will enable the social scientist to "see" such bodies will not be a material object like the old "3-D" red and green eyeglasses, that instantly resolved a jumble of varicolored lines into recognizable images. It will be a principle or series of principles applicable to different levels of analysis according to the phase of human activity with which the particular social science is concerned. Despite the incontestable complexity of human personality some of these principles are found to be surprisingly simple, like the division of matter into animal, vegetable and mineral "kingdoms" and the definition of a chemical element, which helped to get the natural sciences under way, supplanting the old, sub- jectively vivid but objectively meaningless "earth, air, fire and water" formula of medieval alchemy and early quasi-scientific speculation. Some of them may be bewilderingly complex, like the higher mathematical involvements of modern statistical techniques. A danger in the social sciences is that simple means may appear disturbingly akin to those loose, subjective "generalizations" so feared and abominated in the days when history, psychology, economics and sociology were still fighting for recognition as reliably systematic and firmly founded "legitimate" scien- tific disciplines.

The analytical-sensational polarity of style in the plastic arts, associated with the cultural motivations here ascribed to them, may be just such a simple but serviceable generalization. Many well-educated people recall with horror that part of their otherwise enjoyable schooling spent in history classes, but can remember hardly a single one of the weakly linked chain of "facts" they struggled to retain for the final exam. In order to understand a broad area of human experience for general cul- tural orientation, significant generalization is essential. The next few pages will be devoted to a demonstration of the manner in which the present proposals may be used as a "macroscope," not only to determine of what "body" any given work may be a significant part, but also to see some of the broad "3-D" patterns hidden among the jumbled lines of Western European history.

The inclusiveness of the pattern that is being proposed may seem to preclude the practical effectiveness claimed for it as a means of interpret- ing the great variety of actual human attitudes and conduct. It must be remembered, however, that the establishment of the polar categories and their general expressive orientation is just a *beginning,* an instru- mentation for cultural analysis intended to be no more but no less service- able than the "animal, vegetable, mineral" generalization at the basis of the natural sciences, or the "solid, liquid, gas" distinction elementary to an understanding of chemistry. The "macroscope" is focused on the widest possible field in the following pages, simply to demonstrate how it may be used, but the angle can be narrowed for more intensive ex- amination of particular sections.

Another confusion that must be avoided in evaluating analyses of art is the notion that some attempt is being made to substitute the gen- eralization for an experience of the facts. This is the fallacy that has done so much in recent decades to discredit the academic method, partly, to be sure, because the academic method had already fallen into the undeniable trap sufficiently to discredit itself. Academic analysis with its theories, categories, definitions and all the rest of the verbal para- phernalia, must be recognized as a procedure for handling the complexity of experience to some practical end. No mastery of the procedure can have any great value unless its application to experience is understood, is indeed the objective and practice of any intellectual program. To correct a tradition of failure along these lines, it is not advisable to abandon al- together the use of academic analysis or preceptual instruction, but simply to reapply them *more directly to experience.* It would be ludi- crously futile to grasp the reins of a set of carriage harness hanging on a nail in the barn, with the hope of actually getting anywhere. The fact that someone might be foolish enough to do so is no reason for throwing out the harness. To make it handsomely effective, it need simply be thrown over the back and head of a spirited horse and hitched to what- ever sort of rig may be to the purpose of the moment. With all the buckles and straps adjusted and firmly fastened, a man may then hold the reins to some practical effect. Viewed in this way, even the harness maker has a place, though obviously less important than that of the man on the box.

The sequential relation of the polar categories, in which a prior stage of analytical style seems prerequisite to the formation of a sensational style, suggests a cyclical tendency in the evolution of art which must not be taken for granted. It is neither automatic nor entirely inevitable. An analytical style does not give way to a sensational style unless there is some factor in the cultural background favoring change. There is no point at which sensational styles exhaust themselves and allow a new cycle to begin with a return to analytical forms. Such a "recommence- ment" of the cycle occurs only when new conditions arise favoring a new way of life and transferring social, hence cultural control to those who function in a new way. The very first art seems paradoxically to have been basically sensational.

### PREHISTORIC AND ANCIENT ART

Prehistoric art has already been considered here at some length. Fre- quently it has been "written off" as non-art, mere fetishism, so as not to impair the apparent completeness and universality of various cultural theories. Other social sciences have found the cultural practices of primitive societies quite illuminating and this is true also of their expression in art.

Paleolithic naturalism is a sensational expression of insecurity and tension in its fixation on a virtually optic (although slightly linear and mostly planimetric) representation of the most crucial factor in the environment, the hunter's quarry (Plate 1a). Though the nomadic hunting peoples must have had certain established techniques and weapons, however simple, for stalking and killing their prey, their art makes no reference to the human aspects of the hunt comparable in development to the animals themselves. When the hunters appear at all, it is as quasi-symbolic stick figures, with no attempt at the optic reality displayed in depicting the animals. Likewise, considerable knowledge of animal anatomy must have been available to the paleolithic artist, derived from the experience of butchering their carcasses, yet there is no analytical clarification of their bodily structure in the cave paintings. Thus the practical, productive aspects of the hunt are neglected in the consumer's concentration on the quarry, which is constantly expressed by a sensational style of representation.

Neolithic art of abstract geometric design, on the other hand, is in a sense an apotheosis of productive processes (Plate 1b). The relationship between geometric motifs rhythmically spaced, and the manual or structural consequences of the craft processes discussed above (p. 27 ff.) was explored extensively some years ago in the work of the noted anthropologist Franz Boas. Neolithic design is highly analytical in clarity of parts and articulations, rhythmically coordinated. It expresses the first tentative relaxation of mankind's fear of his natural environment, as faith in human capacity to control it and gain security was born with the discovery of elementary principles of agriculture and animal husbandry— what might be called an "arm's length" independence of nature, leading to, but far short of, the confident anthropocentrism that appears finally in Greece.

At the end of the neolithic period, natural forms, sometimes highly distorted or forced into geometric shapes, are used in quasi-pictorial decoration, like Aegean pottery in the "Geometrical Style" and metalwork of the migratory North. This use of human and animal figures in geometrically regulated pattern represents further relaxation of the tension due to human fears about the inhospitality of natural environment. In the North, as is clear from mythology and early literature, such relaxation is far from complete, and animal subjects continue to predominate in this "realistic decoration."

Philosophically, the great river valley or hothouse civilizations at the dawn of history—commonly thought of as Egypt, Mesopotamia, India and China—represent a further transition along this animistic-anthropocentric axis. The mass of mankind was still servile and felt insecure, but the exalted ruler was a godlike character who could deal with the forces of nature and ensure the survival of his faithful subjects. One of the greatest "evidences" of his divine character was his "immortality," to assure themselves of which these civilizations invested untold quantities of human effort and material wealth. The greatest monuments in Egypt were the tombs of the Pharaohs. The temples, if they were not mere funerary adjuncts, were clearly marked as the locus for dealings between the Pharaoh and other divine powers.

The economy of this type of society is basically that of the neolithic community projected quantitatively on a vast scale. Egypt's was a Bronze Age technology, carried doubtless to the highest productivity of which it was capable by the refinements and efficiencies wrought during the careers of generations of master craftsmen. The main reason for the brilliance of these societies, and their greatest difference from the actual neolithic economy, is the vastness of the populations they embraced.

The fact that the Pharaoh was always referred to as the "King of *Upper and Lower* Egypt," and that he wore different ceremonial costumes for performing one or the other of these two roles combined in his own person, seems to support the speculation that a period of consolidation must have taken place just before the beginning of dynastic history. Either because the desiccation of the Sahara, as the last glacier receded, forced the retreating neolithic communities to crowd together in the fertile valley of the Nile, or simply because the process of consolidation led to greater efficiency, wealth and power, there must have been a period in which these communities came into conflict, leading to the subjugation of the weak by the strong. The original privation of simple, natural bounties as the Sahara lost its verdure, succeeded by a more sophisticated community life based on the "knowledge of good and evil," may indeed be reflected in the Scriptural account of the expulsion from Eden.

Success in battle and efficiency in amalgamating the people and property of the defeated groups were dependent on skillful and inspired leadership, which was quickly elevated to divine status. Social, economic and political distinctions between members of the victorious and vanquished groups, as well as between military, religious and productive functions, laid the basis for the caste structure in which the merged populations were controlled. The process must have accelerated after the first "round" or two, when communities thus augmented would have no trouble in absorbing those of more primitive structure, and when the conquest of one advanced group by another would unify "subassemblies" covering a great area. Though there is little historical evidence for such a stage, it may be that no more than two or three generations were required. Similar jobs were done in less time by Alexander the Great, Genghis Khan, Hannibal and Charlemagne. On the other hand, the violence of the process may have been such as to inhibit the growth of cultural refinement for the duration of the struggle, however long it may have been. In any case, it is not until the beginning of dynastic history in the delta and valley of the Nile that the results are clearly visible.

The efficiency in production made possible by increased coordination within the expanded working force, even with little change in the methods employed, created for the few an imposing luxury, to which the proportionately slight quantities of royal and religious paraphernalia that remain bear incontestable witness. The rewards accorded the ruling caste were amply earned by both the spiritual and economic values produced for the community by its coordinating role. Accelerated agricultural production provided sustenance for the necessary quantities of craft labor, and reinforced the sense of economic security which had been introduced by the neolithic way of life. The subservience of the vast population in building pyramids and otherwise glorifying the revered rulers therefore undoubtedly involved elements of loyalty and gratitude. Tendencies of romantic literature and similarly oriented historical pronouncements to deplore the "plight" of the hard-working population as "miserable slavery" cannot accurately convey the spirit that prevailed. The toiling masses must have felt a new sense of security and pride of participation at least in the early stages of the great civilizations at the dawn of history.

Possibly a quaint counsel for the rulers and diplomats of the present may read from this picture of the two final contenders in that great constructive struggle, Upper and Lower Egypt, slugging it out toe to toe as it were, until they arrived at the brilliant solution of uniting under a simple fiction ensuring that neither contender would be submerged. Each would continue autonomous under its own king, only the two kings would both be the same person! Local rulership persisted with a quasi-feudal structure, and in periods of imperial weakness the lower ranks resumed various degrees of independence until new strength at the top brought them again into line.

By and large, except for this rhythm of looser and tighter bonding in the joints accomplished by the last stage or two of the process of amalgamation just outlined, the structure remained constant for about three millennia before the Persian, Greek and Roman conquests, maintaining the rigid caste system characteristic of all the river valley civilizations, which accounts for the comparatively slight degree of cultural change. Insofar as any evolution appears in Egypt, it largely reflects the ebb and flow of social vigor due to the fluctuation of the central dynastic power. In the even longer-lived empires of Asia there is a suggestion of a consumer culture refining itself almost indefinitely, which accounts for the impractical quality of so much Eastern expression, as well as its surpassing lyrical excellence. In impact with the practical West, it has been discovered that the written, and even spoken language in some instances, is quite incapable of conveying practical ideas.

The style of art in Egypt (and likewise the others, perhaps somewhat less clearly) perpetuates in essence the forms of prehistoric expression with great quantitative intensification. Actually the religious art of Egyptian mortuary monuments has something of the naturalism of paleolithic art as it attempts to portray literally a highly mystical, animistic and fearsome cosmology. As in the case of the animals painted by nomadic hunters, the concentration in Egyptian art seems to be upon the forms and factors about which the greatest anxiety was felt; hence the extensive representation of provisions for the ruler's existence in a life after death. A distinct tension in the face of cosmic mystery is expressed by the obvious attempt to fill all available wall space with ritualistic references (Plate 32a). There is little conscious composition, but the arrangement of the material in horizontal banding constitutes some recognition of formal possibilities beyond that of the cave paintings. Great naturalism is exhibited in portraiture for religious use (the *ka* statues, Plate 30a), representations of animals, attendants, and the so-called "ushabti" figurines (Plate 30b). However, in the minor arts and architecture, abstract motifs are combined in simple, insistent rhythms characteristic of neolithic expression (Plate 31a and b). In this type of decorative art, naturalistic forms may also be used, but they are tightly

bound in simple, insistent rhythms, and frequently reduced to geometrical abstraction in which the natural motif may barely be recognizable. Such limitations express the "arm's length" feeling of security from
the wildness of nature that began to appear in the neolithic period.

Thus the culture of Egypt and its reflection in the plastic arts seems
to present both of the familiar attitudes of prehistoric culture, with analytical abstraction characterizing the environment of the living, and
naturalistic representation in mortuary and religious art reflecting mystical attitudes that survived from a more distant past. Although this
pattern of expression was intensified quantitatively during the long
period of the river-valley civilizations, little philosophic reorientation
took place. The evidence of their survival after several millennia, however, may have helped to suggest mankind's dominant role in his natural
environment and the anthropocentrism that followed in Western Europe.

GREECE AND ROME

Not only did the people of ancient Greece take a giant step in achieving the first view of man as the master of his universe, but also in introduc-
ing two related, basic changes in the nature of a work of art. One of
these has already been pointed out: namely, the requirement that every
work of art have both form and content, which has continued to the
present, however much these elements have since been unbalanced
toward abstraction on the one hand, or naturalism on the other. The
second distinction, which still governs the separation of "fine" and
"applied" art, is the development of a substantive independence for
works of the former category.

It must immediately be noted that the boundary between fine and
applied art is sometimes a very difficult line to draw. Even more difficult
is the differentiation between a substantive and a major ancillary work,
especially, for example, in the field of mural decoration. The difference
in form between a processional band of servants on the wall of an
Egyptian tomb, and the processions headed by Emperor Justinian and
the Empress Theodosia in the mosaics decorating the triforium level of
the Church of San Vitale at Ravenna seems on the face of it almost
negligible (compare a and b, Plate 32); but there is an undeniable sense
of cohesion and independence about the latter, confined to a structurally
particular wall space with a sense of compositional limitation, not to be

found in the Egyptian tomb reliefs that seem to be prolonged simply to fill available space.

The precise distinction of a substantive work of art in the modern sense, as it was first developed in Greece for the Western world, is partly that its chief role is to embellish a particular environment. Thus it has a suggestion of free decorative choice, instead of the more compulsive, quasi-fetishistic impact of even the greatest earlier works. Yet it also has meaning, both in terms of the subject represented and the form in which it is cast. The subject may be quite important for the particular site, like the Birth of Athena for one of the pediments of the Parthenon (i.e., the Temple of *Athena Parthenos*) in Athens. But the sensitive application of the figures to the particular space conveys the realization that the work was not produced *simply* to refer to the subject involved, like a Cro-Magnon bison or a servant bearing food in an Egyptian pharaoh's tomb, but also to grace the locality. At the same time, objects created for practical purposes even though embellished with geometrically abstracted designs, as well as with more elaborate pictorial representations, are classed as "minor, or applied" art. To be a work of "fine art" each composition must have some independence *both* of form and content.

The familiar dawn of anthropocentrism in Greece has already been discussed here at some length. An important concomitant of this new concept of man's power is the respect for the potentialities of the individual man simply as a member of the human race, which is evident in the early stages of classical culture both in Greece and Rome. No longer is a god-like ruler the only person of sufficient stature to handle problems of broad social or cosmic scope, to petition or placate the gods. Human beings of all sorts in myths and legends have their dealings with the Olympians. A humanistic democracy is inspired by respect for the native logical equipment of mankind, which is possessed to a degree by all men, and faith in its effectiveness is expressed in the analytical style of the plastic arts in Greece. Later a sensational style develops in the Hellenistic period and in the art of imperial Rome, to reflect the competitive development of individual capacities for exploiting or dominating the social environment.

Sensational style was appropriate to the related Hellenistic and Roman imperial worlds for two reasons. One is that it expressed the luxurious interests characteristic of the consumer as wealth became concentrated in the hands of a small group of commercial and political rulers. The other reason for sensational expression was that its characteristic particularization brought about the novelty and variety of subject matter affording opportunity for the expression of individual differences that became important in a competitive society.

Roman art introduced a distinctive and original aspect of the sensational approach by developing an interest in space, which was extensively used as an element of composition in the imperial period for the first time in the history of art. Spatial composition becomes an integral part of the design of large public buildings, notably the baths (Plate 33a), and illusionistic representation of deep space in environment was quite skillfully accomplished in relief sculpture (Plate 33b), mural painting and mosaics.

With the decline of imperial power, Rome slipped back into the general Mediterranean orbit, and her art, never completely independent of Greece, patterned itself after the new phase of Hellenism, the Byzantine style. Like the fragments of an exploding star in the astronomical universe, certain hints and aspirations for cultural development were spun off from the imperial disintegration into northern Europe, drawing about them local forms and feelings into something quite new and different, somewhat as a spiral nebula is supposed to consolidate material floating in interstellar space into a new celestial body. It was not the abundant physical remains of classical culture throughout her colonies, so much as the spirit of Judaeo-Hellenic Christianity, itself essentially strange to the Roman imperial spirit, that formed the original nucleus of the new cultural development following the arrival of the first missionaries. The more tangible remains of truly classical civilization had to await the growth of a new spirit at a much later date before they again acquired a living cultural meaning in the Renaissance.

### THE MIDDLE AGES: NORTHERN AND EASTERN PHASES

Both Mediterranean and northern European culture in the Middle Ages were dominated spiritually by the other-worldly emphasis of Christianity. For many people, the world was not a pleasant abode during the earlier part, the so-called Dark Ages. Violence in the clash of arms, which had so noble an echo from distant borders during the days of the Empire's glory, had an increasingly terrifying sound as it became a constant local threat to the civic structure, personal property, and even to life itself. The forms of proto-feudal serfdom to which most of the population were doomed as the only means of survival afforded meager subsistence in exchange for incessant labor, and there was no hope for change. Without the army and the brisk trade which it protected in the great days of the Empire, there were no careers in which to escape from the virtual caste system that governed the other areas of life.

The misery and insecurity inflicted upon the vast majority of the population under the moribund empires of the east and west cast them into a despair that seemed to contradict the glorious classical notion of man's personal dignity and superior position in the universe. Indeed it was true that the natural cosmos was every bit as much if not more under his control than it had ever been. The answer that came to be accepted in the name of Christ the Saviour was that the glory of mankind was reserved for the holy and the elect in the life to come. The trials of the flesh provided a test of the spirit, and the thoughts of the blessed must be on the hereafter.

Under such circumstances, of course, the ideal realism of Greek art was mere vanity, for the mortal coil is evil, hence its affliction. The illusionism of Roman art became useless and distracting, for the mind of man must occupy itself in devotional contemplation of that other world, that City of God, rather than waste any attention on his own hopeless and miserable surroundings. The new doctrine was projected by the sophisticated tradition of the Mediterranean world in a form vastly different, as might be expected, from that which it took in the little-tamed wilderness of northern Europe.

In Byzantium's cultural hinterland no void was left by the rupture of Roman hegemony, nor by the ebbing tide of her legions. The Greek world, with its center shifted to Asia Minor during the Hellenistic period, was simply freed of its tributary chains. Its communities and culture continued to flourish about a new capital in Byzantium, renamed Constantinople for the emperor who first rebuilt it to be an alternative seat of the empire as its center of gravity moved eastward. Through periods of success and vitality or disruption and decay, a Greek Byzantium dominated the life of the Mediterranean basin until it was submerged by the Moslem empire of the Ottomans over a thousand years later. Politically and economically the Byzantine world was a projection of the imperialism and luxury developed during the Hellenistic period. Marked changes of taste, however, signify the solidification of a centralized absolutism which replaced the greater political and economic fluidity of the first few centuries following the decline of western or peninsular Greece.

The art of Byzantium abandons the illusionism of Roman (Plate 34a) and Hellenistic art (the former is sometimes considered merely a phase of the latter) in a style which implies no bulk or modeling in its figures and no depth of space in their environment (when any at all is indicated Plates 32b and 34b). This plane character of the murals and icons, and the heavy outlines by which the figures are defined, must not be confused with the linear and planimetric treatment of an analytical style, for they are not used to clarify objective reality or the forms presented. They rather represent a postillusionistic phase of sensational style, in which the artist comes as close as he is permitted by his subject, to an exploitation of the purely aesthetic sensations involved in his work.

The predominant form of monumental art throughout the Byzantine empire was mosaic decoration for church interiors. The brilliant material of this medium is itself the real substance of the works, not any illusionistic or tactile bulk of holy personnages portrayed, which are reduced almost to mere graphological symbols, materially no more than spots in a flat pattern. Thus the retinal *sensations* of pure color and specular reflections of light from the glass surfaces of the mosaic blocks are the true essence of the plastic experience. A realization of the extent to which the material itself enters ino the quality of the sensation derived from a mosaic (as also the pile of a carpet, for example) may be gained from observation that the faces of the blocks are only approximately parallel to the general plane of the work. Imagining the surface perfectly smooth, like a decoration ground flat in a terrazzo floor, the loss of reflected brilliance and textural richness is immediately obvious. (Gold-leafed backgrounds of the icons and parchment pages of the manuscript illumination enter similarly into the aesthetic experience of smaller, more intimate works, for which mosaics of tiny cubes were also used, as in book covers.) It must be noted immediately that Byzantine mosaics have the quality they do, not because they are mosaics, but because they are Byzantine. Roman art had developed great skill in the handling of the mosaic medium before it was handed on to the craftsmen of Byzantium; but the earlier results were highly illusionistic, like the apse mosaic of Sta. Pudenziana, sacrificing the brilliant possibilities of light and color later discovered, to the achievement of a highly convincing representation of tactile form and deep space (Plate 34a).

The heavy Byzantine outlines lack any analytical suggestion of a manual gesture about a three-dimensional form, conveying a quasi-symbolic or pictographic rather than a plastic representation of the intended characters. Their sharp blackness, especially in the icons, sometimes achieves a vibrant contrast of light and dark, consonant with the other elements of aesthetic stimulation already noted. An almost total lack of sculptural production (especially in later centuries of Byzantine culture), further indicates the predominance of optic over tactile concerns.

It may seem at first glance paradoxical that this highly sensational art should express both the upper and lower extremes of a rigid caste system, and its precise relation to opposite ends of the economic scale might be subject to some refinement by close study of the social circumstances. The impoverished multitudes certainly had little opportunity for contact with the elegancies of Byzantine life, even in the religious mosaics. Congregational worship was not practiced in the Eastern Church as in the Church of Rome, which accounts for the small size even of important Eastern churches, like the Cathedral of Athens, which is only about twenty-four feet square. (The gigantic proportions of Hagia Sofia in Constantinople, dating from the beginning of the period, are not typical.)

Byzantine rejection of the objective world reflects the promise of Christianity that salvation and glory await the soul of man in an eternal hereafter. This was partly an appeal to the vestiges of Greek humanism, considerably submerged in the slaves and plebeians, but quite alive for a time among wealthy and educated citizens, who were horrified and indeed often themselves crushed by the corruption and violence in civic life. The sensational style of Byzantine art characteristically expressed disdain for or antagonism against an environment (now the social structure rather than the natural cosmos), which was alike uncomfortable, threatening and mysterious according to the inscrutable fate of birth. Emphasis on celestial authority was intensified in the orthodox Christianity propagated by the patriarchy in Constantinople. Christ was most frequently represented as a completely dominant figure, the Pantokrator or Creator of All Things (Plate 34b). Luxurious aestheticism and hieratic scale are sensational elements of Byzantine style that express autocracy and concentrated power, characteristic of both the secular and religious aspects of Byzantine life.

The usually sophisticated aspects of sensational style, especially in an aristocratic expression, may seem to be absent from the simplified forms of Byzantine mosaic and fresco decoration. Besides the fact that such distinctions are often quite perishable, being more evident to the connoisseurs of their own day, the intrinsic richness of the mosaic medium presented an overawing experience for a vast majority whose living conditions differed little from those of domesticated animals. Also a greater degree of sophistication could be expressed more appropriately in refinements of style found in the more intimate expression of manuscript illumination.

Thus for a thousand years the heir to Alexander's Hellenistic empire continued though wracked by incredible court intrigues and violent successions, as it pursued a somewhat aimless and tortured way, like an old bus on a mountain road. There were times when it sailed gloriously along on smooth downgrades; but on the rocky stretches or uphill pulls it would rattle and puff as though it could not continue much longer. Curiously, what kept the contraption going was not so much attention to the mechanical parts, perhaps foolproof in their simplicity and age like a Model T; but the luxurious formality of the elaborately preserved exterior, asserting a power and glory impressive to the passengers. Despite all its grandeur, the old bus crumpled completely when at last it became involved in a major collision, jammed between a commercially resurgent West, and the Ottoman advance from the East.

*Later Western Emphasis.* Recession of Roman military and commercial activity in the West, however, left a much greater cultural as well as administrative void than in the long civilized East. Roads, cities and governmental organization had not existed there before the penetration of the Roman legions. A near wilderness supported the comparatively sparse population of semimigratory tribes, still goverened partriarchally or by councils of personally autonomous chieftains, whose cultural practices expressed primitive tensions about survival in the natural universe. Religious practice was concerned in large measure with ensuring the "immortality" of deceased leaders, and the arts dealt extensively with animal forms conventionally distorted. A peculiarly northern quality of design appears in a tendency toward flowing linear projection of parts of figures, rather than the distinct, rhythmical association of more clearly geometrical units characteristic of neolithic expression in other areas.

There was little sympathy or cultural exchange between such primitive expression and the anthropocentric naturalism of Roman art. Except for a later elite of Romanized barbarians, conqueror and conquered maintained their separate social strata and cultural independence much as did Asiatic cultures during the recent centuries of European imperial domination. However, when Christian zeal started to missionize northern France, western Germany, Britain and Ireland about the eighth century, the primitive tribesmen recognized a more sophisticated expression of the mystery and tensions they had felt regarding their natural environment, and readily accepted it with a strong blend of their own sympathetic practices and beliefs. A special attraction of Christianity, of course, was the assurance that the rewards of the hereafter were open to all men of good faith, not alone the rulers and those attached to their persons. Thus the humanistic transformation of neolithic culture in the north was neither as complete nor as spontaneous as in Greece, but an importation of the derivative and compromised humanism of Christianity.

Plastic expression in the north, like its population and economic substance, was extremely sparse for a number of centuries, but a few of the more wealthy and powerful monasteries dedicated some of their human resources to a brilliant tradition of manuscript illumination. They found the ingeniously complex, flowing motifs of the Asiatic wanderers highly suitable for expressing their zealous, ecstatic devotional tensions about the mystery of salvation. The endlessly swirling "interlaces and lacertines" of Hiberno-Saxon manuscript illumination, used to elaborate initial letters almost to the full size of the page, to fill complex borders, and work whole pages into turbulent cross designs, express the anxious fullness of heart of men "running scared" toward a goal of mystic salvation (Plate 20). Each twist and turn of the complicated design is the monastic artist's devout reassertion of his love of God and hope for eternal blessedness, such as his brothers would make in prayers repeated over and over for hours on end, or in each plodding step of a pilgrimage to Rome. Even in secular manuscripts, however, or in those for which Charlemagne specified a style in imitation of ancient Roman illusionism, drapery is swirled, outlines are jagged, in a manner reflecting the nervous activity which is a constant ethnic or local characteristic of northern art.

Western Europe, whose people had glimpsed the power and glory of age-old Mediterranean culture through the life and structures of local capitals and outposts established by the Romans throughout Spain, France and Britain, was in a sorry state at the outset of Charlemagne's career. Movement was cut off to the north by the depredations of piratical, seafaring Scandinavians, and to the south by the incursions of the Moors through Spain up into southern France, and across the Mediterranean to Sicily and southern Italy. There was no incentive for miserable people, practicing primitive agricultural techniques, to increase their efforts for a greater yield, which would be taken from them either by their own overlords or stronger enemies. The seemingly complete surrender of personal rights in the bonds of serfdom to which the individual acceded in this extremity is almost incomprehensible to the present era of thorough individualism. It is an index of the frightful situation which faced the peaceful, working population.

As the last vestiges of all that human cooperation had gained in the struggle for existence seemed to be slipping away, people realized its inestimable value and were willing to yield anything for the protection of the least social organization against the hazards of elemental nature and the violence of predatory men. It was to the community that personal rights were sacrificed, not to the person of the leader who would direct it. (Of course, many of those who accepted the yoke of serfdom had never known freedom. They were slaves on the great Roman latifundia, or members of the migratory hordes where a patriarchal allegiance was traditional.) Violence did not immediately cease, but as it was drawn within bounds, the productive and protective functions of the manorial system became increasingly formal and automatic. Thus there was no longer any practical challenge to stimulate the hereditary leaders and maintain their effectiveness. Assured their positions by birth, the knights and barons continued to enjoy, expand, and in some instances to abuse their privileges immune from restraint, by virtue of their "dues" and military control.

## GROWTH OF CITIES

The beginnings of change are attributed to the reversal of two factors inhibiting movement and trade. Charlemagne managed to unite a feudal hegemony of sufficient strength to expel the Moors from Europe, opening up the south and access to the Mediterranean Sea, while the Vikings began to favor peaceful commerce instead of continual "hit and run" raids, setting up regular channels by sea across the north of Europe and by land southward. They opened up the Eastern wilderness in an attempt to establish communication with Byzantium, thus starting the growth of the Russian nation. The added range of travel permitted a floating population of Jews and other outcasts to carry with them objects of trade from distant places which had more advanced techniques in the crafts. Local agriculture throughout Europe was stimulated to produce surpluses to barter for such objects, new lands were claimed from the wilderness and the rotation of the fallow was changed from the two-field to the three-field system, increasing by half the yield from the land already in use. Production and trade stimulated one another in a vast eruption of highways, markets and new market towns populated by free, self-governing merchants and craftsmen.

The town replaced the manor as the center of socioeconomic organization in the new market economy. The doors of opportunity were flung open to the freedman and the artisan. Feudal aristocracy fought for survival by forceful containment of the new growth where that could be accomplished, elsewhere by rendering appropriate services to the new activity in towns and "communes"—military protection and development of trade routes and market centers, gradual expansion of political units in order to widen the scope of commercial operations, and rudimentary functions of constructive market regulation. Some of the aristocracy were sufficiently adaptable to turn to advantage their position and wealth in various phases of the new commerce; but concessions to progress gradually brought forth new ways, new leaders and new thoughts on every hand.

The dawn of individual opportunity in the market radically changed the dominant philosophy of life, and the evolution of a new cultural expression perfectly reflects the process. First, a great increase in artistic production occurred in the Romanesque period, about the first two centuries of the second Christian millennium, in which a new clarity and consistency of purpose is apparent although still in terms of the traditional other-worldly ideology. Interesting isolated instances of a kind of genre naturalism appeared at this time in Romanesque historiated capitals (Plate 35a and b), and a similar spirit is felt in the attempts at literal narrative pictorialization in the tympanums of the main portals at Vézelay (*Descent of the Holy Spirit,* Plate 35c) and Autun (*Last Judgment.*) By the Gothic period (beginning in the thirteenth century) a slightly idealized presentation of natural form was the recognized technical objective (Plate 36b), and narrative elaboration of the subject was generally practiced. Cathedral churches built by financial contributions of burghers proud of their community's wealth became the outstanding ecclesiastical monuments of the Gothic period, supplanting in importance the abbeys of the great monasteries.

Subject matter also changed in accord with the spreading concern for material welfare and the interest in individual qualifications of persons capable of making a constructive contribution to the common endeavor. The personal life of Christ was depicted rather than His hieratic eminence, with increased attention paid to the story of the Passion. A growing emphasis on the Virgin Mother, whose life became the subject of the main portals of the thirteenth century cathedrals as at Amiens and Reims, and on saints personally related to particular worshipers (by name, trade, locality, sex, and so on) as intercessors, guardians or confidants, indicates that salvation was conceived increasingly as an individual problem. It was hard for the successful merchant and craftsman, who saw his efforts clearly contribute to the welfare and happiness of those about him, to believe himself so far behind the least of them in God's love. Conscientiously bestowing devout homage and generous benefactions in God's name, he could not feel that his life would merit eternal damnation for its fleshly comfort, were its pious dedication *adequately witnessed* before the throne of God. The need in an increasingly complex and interdependent world to relate morality as well as faith to salvation eventually produced the Reformation, and inspired the Italian Renaissance to revive the authority of ancient classical humanism.

Here, obviously, is a change in the way of life which inspired a vast change in the thoughts and feelings of society, and should be reflected clearly in the style of its plastic expression. It is, indeed. Discounting a modern view of the inherited other-worldly subject matter of Romanesque art (which, as just indicated, is for its own time less abstract and mystical than what had gone before) ample stylistic evidence of a "recommencement" of the sequence of polar categories can be found. Romanesque style is practically the first indigenous northern expression in historic times, excepting possibly related immediate forerunners like the manuscript illumination already discussed, production of which was too sparse and scattered to be considered a full-blown, thoroughly homogeneous style. Although Romanesque forms in the north often show flowing, involved movement, this is due to the unclarifying ethnic tendency of northern styles toward sensational material (Plate 35c), and does not appear in southern Romanesque styles, as at St. Trophime in Arles, where proportions are heavier and less movement is displayed (Plate 36a). Compositions are analytical in contrast with the Gothic style that follows, the Romanesque being characterized by more discrete association of parts and more shallow, planimetric depth of relief and movement. There is almost no concept of spatial environment about the rhythmically isolated figures in the tympanum at Moissac, and all compositional relations between figures in those of Vézelay and Autun are strictly parallel to the relief plane.

The liveliness which may appear naïve in a symbolic figure like the "dancing" Apostle on the trumeau at Moissac, can be interpreted as a step toward revivifying religious dogma, hence a reduction of the mystical impracticality sometimes indiscriminately associated with apocryphal religion, especially throughout the Middle Ages. Mysticism may be considered categorically impractical only when it involves rejection of known logical or scientific methods and explanations. The high degree of naturalism eventually accomplished in Gothic art is for its time an advance toward illusionism clearly signalizing interest in the nature and affairs of the world. In relation to Romanesque style it is an optic, sensational expression which evolved out of the interest of Romanesque artists in the work-a-day world, shown especially in works like historiated capitals. Minor locations of this sort were doubtless omitted from official specifications of subject matter, and in many buildings conventional decorative forms are used. Occasionally, however, the masons gave rein to their imaginations, and lively representations of Scriptural narrative appear, as well as genre scenes such as beekeeping, hunting, milling, wine making and glass blowing.

The more analytical character of Romanesque composition also is found in architecture, especially in the plan and structure of the cathedrals and abbeys, which are built as a cluster of separate units (narthex, nave, transepts, apsidal chapels, Plate 17a), whereas in the Gothic period they are fused into an approximately rectangular plan, and internal structural divisions are minimized in the interest of unified continuity of space. As previously noted, the Gothic narthex and transepts no longer project beyond the limits of the side aisles; radiating chapels around the apse merge into a continuous contour at a radius extending only to the façade of the shortened transepts (Plate 17b); and on the interior, stilting and pointing of the arches level the nave vaulting into a continuous, cellular whole instead of the isolated series of bays produced in the earlier churches by domed rib vaults with semicircular arches.

Despite the development of new fortunes and new paths to power in the crafts and trade, the old feudal aristocracy managed to retain considerable wealth and station, insofar as individual local rulers were flexible enough to serve the expanding needs of the market, or brutal enough to exact tribute by force. Especially in Italy, where military aspects of feudalism were inherited by the city-state along with other long-established patterns of institutional power, greater opportunity than elsewhere was open to individual tyrants or dynasties like those of the Medici, Sforza, and Piccolomini families. Individuals of outstanding military and political abilities were able to use inherited social position to further the scope of their patrimonies. The men who won new power for such dynasties were of course energetic, decisive, keenly aware of the developments going on around them and the nature of the opportunities they offered. The art which so many of them generously supported as an indication of wealth and civic importance has the intensely analytical character of Florentine *quattrocento* (fifteenth century, i.e., the "four hundreds") naturalism, by contrast with the luxurious sensational styles of the later Baroque, and it grew naturally out of and beside Gothic realism. As against early medieval art, however, this new realism in its detailed imitation of anatomy and unified spatial composition foreshadows the rise of an increasingly optic style.

Admiration for classical example in the success and beauty of its realism, and also in order to cite a revered authority in support of humanistic intellectual inquiry against the opposition of the Church and its Inquisition, spread rapidly in the fifteenth century, which saw among other classical references the first nude and the first equestrian portrait in free-standing sculpture since ancient times, in the *David* and the *Gattamelata* of Donatello. As local power was consolidated in the sixteenth century, the great families converged on Rome in a struggle to extend their dynastic scope. Such eminence required an expression beyond too easy vulgar grasp, so the Renaissance was taken from the craftsmen and inventors, and turned over to the scholars.

The wealthy families formed collections of antiquities and libraries of ancient manuscripts. Not the light, but the letter of ancient practice became the guide of Renaissance culture, and after a briefly brilliant Golden Age producing the gigantic genius of Raphael, Michelangelo and Titian, the academic and highly sensational period of the Baroque ensued, and the decline of Italy's cultural leadership began. Previous discussion (p. 97 ff.) has dealt with the aristocratic significance of sensational style, and the correspondence is so plain in Italian Baroque art that no further elaboration is necessary.

## GROWTH OF NATIONS

The process of national unification, clearly foreshadowed in the growth of the Italian city-state, eventually undermined the vestigial feudal powers wielded by the dukes and barons as military tyrants, though many of their titles have persisted to the present day. At first nations were ruled by absolute monarchs whose positions were due nominally to feudal rights, but actually due to support from the townspeople in whose interest they were supposed to control the predatory excesses of the nobility and promote various forms of efficiency in national unification. The merchants and manufacturers found it better to assume the burden of regular taxation to support national services like the promotion of uniformity in language, currency and commercial measurements, and a standing army to limit piracy, rather than to risk ruin in catastrophic visitations either of local or foreign "men on horseback." Machiavelli proposed the unification of Italy in his famous plan submitted to a Medici pope, Leo X, and the German cities had their powerful, proto-national Hanseatic League; but Italy and Germany, leaders of Europe in the age of cities, were surpassed by France, England, Spain and Holland as new patterns emerged in the age of nations, and France became the active cultural leader of the Western world, except for a period of brilliant production in Spain and Holland at the very outset.

The art of France demonstrates the correspondence of cultural expression to a distinct pattern of human activity, since two parallel styles, practiced throughout the monarchy, reflected divergent interests of the two parties in the ill-mated national alliance. The self-centered culture of the court broke away for a brief moment of brilliant fantasy from the stream of bourgeois realism, just as the doctrine of the "divine right of kings" sought to ignore the facts of contemporary political and economic life, only to perish in the violence of the French Revolution which it provoked. Francis I, an intense admirer of the Italian Renaissance, started its spread throughout Western Europe as the hallmark of nobility and power in one national court after another with his School of Fontainebleau. In the seventeenth-century style of Poussin a genuinely analytical interest is expressed, not with the exhaustive linear clarity of fifteenth-century Italian naturalism, but rather as of the sixteenth century with a suggestion of Raphael in figure compositions and the Venetian artists in landscape (Plate 27a). The extremes of academic classicism were gradually submerged in the posturing sophistication of the Poussiniste-Rubeniste polemics, and aristocratic expression in the eighteenth century assumed a highly sensational style, showing an almost complete rejection of practical concern. The erotic, bombastic or flippant painting of Boucher (Plate 37b) and others at the courts of the Louis' truly reflects the philosophy of political absolutism and the meaning of Marie Antoinette's proverbial "let them eat cake." Divine right as a doctrine reflects the sense of entrenchment expressed by a sensational style in art. Marie's oft repeated inanity reveals complete unawareness and detachment from the practical situation.

At the same time the realistic tradition of the Gothic period carried forward by the Van Eycks, Breughel and the seventeenth-century Dutch masters in the north, the Naturalists, Caravaggio and later *"bambocianti"* in Italy, and Georges du Mesnil de Latour (Plate 37a) and the Le Nain brothers in seventeenth-century France itself, inspired or culminated in the genre and still life painting of Chardin; and a brisk trade flourished in the work of a host of nameless craftsmen, many of them emigrants from the Low Countries, where bourgeois cultural expression had been freest and least interrupted. In subject matter, these works continued to represent actual aspects of the life of their times, but with growing emphasis on its less practical phases as the style became increasingly more optic. Unpretentious in size, they were sold "over the counter" as it were, in the fairs and markets of the Left Bank like any other article of commerce, at the same time that grandiose works in the rococo style were painted for the aristocracy on commission by honored and socially acceptable Academicians.

Given free rein after the eighteenth century by release from the political and social supremacy of the nobility, the expression of bourgeois individualism burgeoned at an ever accelerating pace. Romanticism, aestheticism and abstraction in turn carried plastic expression to new extremes of sensational form and virtually complete rejection of all objective representation or concern. A genuinely analytical expression appeared at the outset in the highly linear styles of David (Plate 38a) and Ingres, followed by the slightly more optic realism of Courbet. Romanticism under the leadership of Eugene Delacroix proceeds to a sensational use of chiaroscuro and broken color (Plate 38b), but many of his contemporaries, like Gérôme and Géricault, clung to a more clarified and tactile style as in his own early *Liberty on the Barricades* or *The Death of Sardanapalus*. The "boulevard realism" of Manet and Degas (Plate

7), as well as pleine-airism of the Barbizon school and the impressionists, are various aspects of a quite sensational illusionism, the latter pointing the way to subsequent aestheticism of the postimpressionists and twentieth-century abstraction (Plate 44b).

Many particular factors influenced the styles of various artists in this period of apparently kaleidoscopic individualism, but the gradual trend away from any practical interest toward thoroughly sensational form is the greatest force in each artist's attempt to be different from others. These characteristics of nineteenth- and twentieth-century style reflect the social prominence of the successful entrepreneur, and the complete financial independence of his descendants, made possible by the new efficiency and fluidity in the organization of financial capital. In no previous age have so many been able to pursue leisure and luxury to so complete a degree.

Although a modicum of practical expression may be found here and there in the plastic arts during the nineteenth century, it has been virtually eliminated in the internationally accepted Parisian aestheticism of the twentieth century, emulated with official approval in America. The growth of "documentary realism" in other arts, however, reflects an expansion of political and economic democracy, almost unrecognizable in painting and sculpture. Highly aestheticized form and complete rejection or obscure distortion of reality have transformed the plastic arts into a medium for highly refined and socially exclusive expression, following almost a century and a half of retreat from reality begun in the historical and geographical remoteness of Romantic subject matter. Pressure for novelty causes the artist to "experiment" with so many new suggestions that frequently the emotional and sensuous phases of post-illusionistic sensationalism appear in the same work, as in many examples by Klee, Van Gogh, and Chagall (Plate 44a).

The apparent chaos and contradiction of the current cultural scene reflect a fluidity in the socioeconomic structure no longer susceptible of description in terms of rigid patterns of social status. It is necessary to recognize that socially oriented practical concerns as well as self-centered enjoyment of luxury are combined, though in vastly varying degrees, in every modern personality. Cultural manifestations can now best be understood as composite expressions of the interests of "producers" and "consumers," in a manner to be discussed at length in the following section.

EMERGENCE OF CULTURAL DISTINCTION BETWEEN
PRODUCER AND CONSUMER

Suggestions thus far regarding choices between analytical and sensational modes of expression, made on the basis of the relatively practical or
nonpractical interests of the patronizing society, have emphasized contrasts between the concerns of rulers and ruled, between aristocratic and
plebeian tastes. With the coming of the Industrial Revolution and its
consequences in the commercial, financial and political reorganization of
Western society, inherited status lost nearly all importance for cultural
analysis, and society became so flexible that categorical distinctions of
cultural interest can no longer be made with any degree of certainty in
terms of social position. The son of a tycoon may become a scientist or a
philanthropist as well as a racing enthusiast or a stage-door johnny; he
may be given a bankrupt railroad to reorganize as a present for his twenty-
first birthday, or he may become the tactical genius of world-wide
mergers, trade penetrations or acquisition of raw materials for a corpora-
tion founded by his father or grandfather. Sons of poor immigrants buy
fabulous collections of old and modern masters, and some wives of
moderately successful dress manufacturers and advertising executives
are concerned with less practical activities than the widow of a "patri-
cian" President of the United States.

Patrons of art respond to one or the other pole of cultural expression
according to the immediacy and degree of their contact with production
and the struggle for control of its earnings. Analytical form expresses the
point of view of producers, because it arises from practical impulses
necessary to such activity. Sensational form expresses the relatively
passive, critical role of the consumer, concerned with an instantaneous
sensory appraisal of cultural forms that offer entertainment through
movement and sensation. With the prevalence of artistic examples from
previous ages available in the highly coordinated modern world, however, and large numbers of producers and consumers simultaneously in
a position to enjoy and even acquire works of art, there is no longer
clearly apparent the process of evolution from one stage to another. Both
types of art are in constant, though perhaps unequal demand. Any
tendency toward evolution is apt to occur rather in the taste of a particular individual passing from one economic role to another, although
of course some people are trained to a sophisticated, sensational taste
from childhood.

The distinction between bourgeois or plebeian and aristocratic taste before about 1800, when they existed simultaneously but remained independent as expressing quite different sections of society, must be replaced after that date by the much more fluid and overlapping categories of "producer and consumer." It is no longer possible to designate the age or even an entire social group as subscribing to one or the other category of taste exclusively. Indeed, current public confusion in the arts has resulted from attempts of the different "schools" to insist arbitrarily on the universal superiority of their own standards. The layman is at a loss to choose between the authorities advocating academic taste, which he may find sympathetically analytical and clear, but dull (see above under Eclecticism, p. 111 ff;) and those that insist on sensational "avant-gardisme," which he may find obscure and excessively bizarre.

No such ambiguity confused people's cultural attachments before the Industrial Age. When dynastic succession obtains, a person is either "born to the purple" or he is not, and unalterable conditions of birth determine the entire structure, whatever may have been the "legitimist" struggles that frequently arose. Certain rulers, to be sure, have been more energetic and practical than others, but the taste and role of each were closely identified in Western European society with the historical stage of their dynasty's development. Since the growth of mass industry, bringing about finance capital and the rise of the entrepreneur, however, outward appearances may show little direct correlation between the obvious material factors constituting an individual's wealth and power, and his personal quality or cultural attitude. The process of commercial escalation can be so rapid that opposite types of interest seem frequently to merge in the same individual. Indeed, the producer-consumer polarity describes extremes of personality of which few, if any, pure examples exist. This phase of the distinction requires further examination.

Although it might be possible for a consumer to have no practical impulses or capacities whatsoever, every producer *has to be* a consumer at least insofar as he eats and drinks substances among which he is bound to feel *some* preferences, and enjoys the protection of clothing and shelter in which *some* distinction of comfort and attractiveness must be obvious even to the most indifferent. Among present-day wage earners, however, a doctor or a factory worker may be sufficiently concerned with the pursuit of intangible values to paint pictures on Sunday or subscribe to an orchestral series. Indeed some show of concrete cultural interest is expected throughout the professional world and likewise to some extent among higher ranking business executives.

Similarly, there are few pure consumers. A completely independent coupon clipper may pioneer in an important scientific field or enjoy the less responsibly practical activity of tinkering with speedboats or antique automobiles, while flightier social peers will flee even the most mildly practical concerns in pursuit of sheer entertainment.

From such examples it is clear that the beginnings of economic democracy which have been won from the industrial machine in the recent past, such as the eight-hour day, paid vacations and earnings sufficient for a standard of living well above subsistence levels, have made it possible for many *productive* workers in industry and the professions to devote considerable attention to the functions of *consuming* goods and services. Many people in the common walks of life have developed a substantial interest and capacity in choosing what they buy for aesthetic quality as well as for practical value, for greater comfort and embellishment in their lives. At the same time, finance capital with its coupons and dividends has made possible complete divorcement from the necessity of contact with productive activity for a larger group of *pure consumers* than ever before in the history of mankind. To determine their respective interests in art, and especially to dispel confusions that have arisen from the consumer-connoisseur's arrogation to himself of the role of universal critic and final arbiter of values in the arts, it is necessary to identify the attitudes that correspond with the functions of producing and consuming.

*Production* of any sort requires regular procedures, repeated exactly or with slight progressive improvement, according to a clear logic of applying familiar means to precisely purposed ends. For any given intelligence there must be one "best" way of doing a thing, and if the object is production—getting it done—it would be absolutely pointless and unthinkable to change to a different way unless a new "best" were discovered, permanently supplanting the old. Considerations of novelty, sensation, mystery are extraneous to the business of serious production, and serve the personality of the producer only in minor, playful aspects of his personal activity. A producer's sense of power and security in his environment derives from his practical skill in controlling it, which he clearly understands. On this basis he is able to construct a genuinely humanistic attitude toward the capacities of mankind and the worth of his fellow men, devoid of excessive anxiety about the adequacy of his own performance or soundness of its direction.

For the pure *consumer* type or phase of personality there is no logic but the choice of the moment. No need to inquire how a thing is built or prepared; just taste it, feel it, sit and watch it. If it appeals to that sophisticated intuition which is the residue or distillation of many previous *sensations* of similar objects and experiences, it can be purchased by a simple act of will. Subjective evaluation of this sort, unlimited by practical considerations, will tend to vary as the consumer's desires and tastes change from waking morn to weary night, from flaming youth to flagging age, and indeed repetition tends to become meaningless and oppressive without the logic of productive necessity. Novelty then assumes a positive value to awaken the attention and the senses, which are not concerned with assessable practical values.

People who find themselves in such a position of willful power cannot fully respect the general run of mankind who must serve them so absolutely. With time, as in the case of aristocratic succession, the inevitable question, "Why am I so much more comfortably maintained than they who do the world's work?" must unconsciously plague the hearts of many unproductive heirs to the great commercial fortunes. Subconscious tensions regarding the continuity of their power due to these misgivings are intensified by any personal frustration, and by the swiftness of change that is the constant threat of commercial competition. The unprobing acceptance of appearances, characteristic of sensational style in art, or the nonobjectivity of postillusionistic sensationalism (See p. 37) are appropriately diverting under such conditions. Sophisticated style, moreover, must bear constant witness by means of an elegance and complexity fully comprehended only by the elite, to the superiority of its patrons, who can no longer point even to an anachronistic fiction of superior birth.

From another angle it may be observed that the practical reaction of the producer faced with a problem is not to express how he *feels* about it, but to determine and undertake what he must *do* about it. The consumer, on the other hand, utters his *feelings* (often with exaggerated emotion, tension or anxiety, due in part to his inability to gauge the practical dimensions of any given problem) virtually as a command to others to strive for a solution that will please him. This is also the technique of primitives in one sense and of children in another, in their attempts to control an environment they can only dimly understand.

The ritual "magic" of one and the tantrum of the other are both intensely expressed *wishes* for something they feel incapable of attaining directly by their own power and skill.

During those periods in which new leaders have integrated new patterns of social organization, whether in respect to production, distribution or community functions, an analytical expression of their highly practical role in society has always been developed in the arts. When inheriting generations have felt no further need of making a personal contribution in order to win or maintain their position of social control and its attendant privileges, their concern has shifted to a career of deriving the greatest personal satisfaction from ingenuity and sophistication in *spending* their wealth. Managers of all types, from the palace mayor of ancient kings to the corporate management of invested capital, have isolated their employers from the practical demands of the enterprises that produce their wealth, leaving the latter free to spend their time and talents in choosing goods or engaging in pastimes invented for their delight.

"I like this, let's have it. This is fun, let's do it," is virtually the limit of the practical considerations involved for the consumer. Heightened sensation, dynamic novelty is offered to a particular personality that judges not by analytical calculation, but by reference to a developed "taste" modified according to the mood of the moment. The arts become an important area for the exercise of such acquisitiveness, which is precisely expressed in the sensuous emphasis and freedom from practical limitation (e.g., open composition, unclarified structure) of a sensational style.

The actual process of creating a work of art for such taste confers somewhat the same role of selector on the artist himself. Instead of proceeding progressively, step by step, according to a craft formula in which all means are directed toward definite ends as in an early, analytical stage, there is a tendency for an artist creating a sensational expression to "try" things that appeal to him. He stands back and studies each bit of paint, assays its relation to the total effect of the work, modifies the result this way and that, impulsively, subjectively, until he "gets" something that satisfies him. The growth of the slowly drying, hence extensively alterable oil medium was due to the rise of this sensational approach, and is associated also with a search for "accidental" values. When the artist does not like what he has done, he may take out portions or discard the whole thing and start afresh. Thus the artist himself alternates the role of consumer-critic with that of producer, becoming less and less practical in his creative approach.

Artists on the whole became shockingly ignorant of their craft by the end of the nineteenth century, and media requiring fairly extensive technical knowledge, like sculpture, mural painting and the graphic arts, were for a time looked down upon by easel painters, who felt the product of *their* less fettered spirits must be categorically superior. This attitude has since undergone some change, especially in the United States, where the interest of many artists in achieving a wide audience was favored by the opportunities of the federal art program of the thirties in the mural and printing mediums. The bizarre concern of many artists recently with material aspects of their work, however, such as constructing their works out of rags and rubbish, on one hand, or the latest plastic resins and esters, on the other, is obviously inspired by a search for aesthetic novelty rather than practical invention.

*Pretensions and Obscurity in Art Criticism.* Progress will not be made understanding the complexities of cultural expression, nor will forms be provided to relieve current neglect of the producer's taste in the plastic arts, as long as so many people refuse to accept categorization of their artistic taste that implies any limitations whatsoever. There is a widespread tendency to insist that the big "I" is equipped with all the capacities accessible to mankind, or that the missing ones are not only unimportant but that their exclusion is necessary to higher achievement, like the celibacy of the clergy. Qualified critics are afraid to admit openly any important reservations about a style that is popular with the connoisseur. Laymen are cowed by implications of abysmal rusticity that have been attached to the expression, ". . . . but I know what I like," and abjectly surrender their God-given right to be direct and simple. Those who cultivate or pretend to a more informed taste resent any suggestion that it might have parochial limitations, however elegant or exalted, refusing to admit the validity toward other ends of more obvious and appealing forms of expression.

Perhaps this blindness to the finite aspects of any given taste is akin to the problem psychiatrist Carl Jung saw when he pointed out the need for a person to discover and accept his "shadow." The conservative, academic person refuses to admit in his attitude any lack of sophistication or spiritual agility. The sophisticate refuses to admit any superficiality or condescension toward his fellow man. Everyone wants to "be himself" in whatever colors may happen to strike his fancy; but he insists on *seeing* himself and being seen as draped in a rainbow superiority that blends, under such prevalence, merely into an unexceptionable gray.

Many people who are informed about the plastic arts, accepting much of the aestheticism of modern abstraction, resist the interpretation of such styles as an expression primarily of privileged, self-centered people with no practical concerns. They resent being classified with rentiers and consumers, and cite various intellectual fields in which they may be well informed and socially oriented. Close examination of such a person generally reveals that one or the other horn of the balance is quite light. His interest in sensational expression may have been dutifully cultivated because it is fashionable and challenging, a pleasant entertainment when there is so little of a more practical nature to compete for his attention. The averred "practicality" of one who finds genuine satisfaction in ultrasophistication must represent a very limited phase of his activity, or a pose affected to avoid conflict with a popular American prejudice.

An antagonism to various aspects of aristocracy has grown throughout the Western world in the nineteenth century with special overtones in America. The "land of opportunity" has firmly eliminated all requirements other than energy and ability to qualify contestants in the race for success. A fierce rejection of older and less relevant attributes has resulted in making people feel almost ashamed of a favorable economic and social background, or at least in reducing the recognition of whatever success they may have accomplished. In certain contexts there is a suspicion of immorality attached to wealth and power without an appropriate "rags to riches" background, which seems to serve as a sort of *ex post facto* kind of penance.

Whatever his private feelings, everyone insists publicly on a high evaluation of the common touch. Actually, a wide awareness and deep appreciation of human quality at all levels of society is primarily characteristic of the creative, producing stage of a new society, or of productively oriented individuals on the more heterodox modern scene. When it is falsified for the purposes of politics and trade by those whose functions and attitudes have rejected this stage, serious confusions in cultural interpretation result. Thus in the plastic arts, where the prevalence of high costs per unit and other economic factors tend to confine purchases to the wealthy (unless some sort of community patronage exists), the taste of the producer is pushed into a secondary position, or virtually eliminated. The consumer characteristically takes the position that his taste is superior and ultimate. Once he collected costly old masters; and this is still done, largely as a means of investment; but now he often insists on relegating all that has gone before to the scrapheap and disqualifying those who reject his extravagant standards from the circle of complete human personality. Hence, for example, the revolting connotations that often attach to the word "vulgar," or the condescension once implied in the term "chromo." Art historians will probably never cease to deplore the destruction of a series of fine fifteenth-century frescoes in the nave of Santa Maria Novella in Florence, to make way for the more "sophisticated" altarpieces by Vasari, which are now considered utterly banal.

To correct this sort of prejudice it is necessary not only to grant the fitness of analytical style for expression of the perfectly dignified social stage or individual role of producer; but it is also necessary to absolve the consumer attitude from automatic condemnation as parasitical, self-ish and ruinous. Such accusations must be launched only against *excesses* of capriciousness and obscurity in sensational expression, for a considerable element of refinement and fantasy is necessary to a genuinely human personality. African Pygmies, whose economy is so marginal that virtually all their energies must be employed in the mere effort to survive, might be considered examples of the complete producer; but they have developed almost no formalized culture at all, and their lives can hardly be considered attractive.

Both poles have their own values, and one or the other must predominate in order to confer legible homogeneity on a given work of art; but it is only impoverished by unnecessary antagonism to any expressive quality in the name of an arbitrary purity, perfection or refinement. The ideal, of course, is the society or personality that remains practical, constantly intensifying understanding and control of environment, but at the same time dedicating the resultant power and wealth to greater refinement and enjoyment of living, i.e., to the functions of consuming. The two objectives are not mutually exclusive, provided they are sensitively adjusted. In fact such combination of interests is precisely the description of human personality in a so-called "Golden Age," described above as characterizing "transitions of growth."

Thus far the comparatively rare phenomenon of the Golden Age has been an accident of historical evolution. But with adequate development of the nascent social sciences, it should become a constant social objective, attainable a great part of the time. This would require chiefly that humanity recognize the dangers inherent, on the one hand, of pursuing too ardently the beguilements of the consumer role, of rejecting too completely the limitations and responsibilities of productive discipline. On the other hand, the producers or their representatives in the cultural professions must refrain from decrying all innovation, all departure from clearly reasonable formulae as "sheer insanity." In other words, any given mode of cultural expression must serve as a proud and self-confident badge of identification for its inventors instead of being contentiously advanced as a program to be imposed on all.

*Education for the Golden Age.* To make this possible, of course, some adjustment must be made in widely prevalent social practices, including the educational procedures whereby the rising generation is introduced to the complexities of life. The time-honored method has been to drill the child rigorously in the elements of various techniques, broken down to a point where his attention presumably can encompass them. This has worked well enough in productive stages of society or in vocational training of productive skills, because the processes of production and the attitudes generated when it is the dominant cultural concern are characterized by a clarity and delimitation that are susceptible of analysis and sequential attention. Several decades ago it became evident that this left something to be desired as preparation for the increasingly dominant consumer personality in modern culture. The initial reaction of one school of educational thought, to ignore all rules, eliminate all methodical instruction, was found, however, not to be the best answer.

Practical content has been restored to the educational process in varying degrees under several theoretical justifications. One has not been adduced, however, that might seem more complete and illuminating than the others. It follows from the cultural analysis presented above. Since in the evolution of human culture it may be observed that a sensational expression has only been evolved (with one notable exception to be discussed forthwith) upon the basis of a prior analytical expression, whose techniques it must employ and whose ideals constitute the norm on which later sophistications are elaborated, it might be advisable for the educational process to conduct the child through the prior analytical stage (without, of course, the implications of finality that academic education has too often insisted upon in the past) so that any sophistication he may eventually achieve may be better founded, more richly structured.

In this way, those not destined for a highly sensational, consumer's role in life would be provided, as far as they might go, with appropriately analytical equipment serviceable for a practical life, and not with a strange, incomplete and frustrated proto-sophistication of no use to them at all. An educational program of this sort might eliminate some of the disciplinary problems in schools today, by more effectively arousing the interests of the majority of students. At the same time, institutions of higher education would be provided with better qualified and more receptive entering classes. A serious distortion arises from current emphasis on being "in the know," of being "hep" to special knowledge that is either more subtle, devious or privileged than that generally available. As a result students actually resist straightforward, basic information as unnecessary or as belittling their status as insiders, "hipsters" or the like.

To vocationalize secondary education is not at all what is advocated in this connection. If such a program were limited to particular groups it would be grossly undemocratic. If nothing more were offered it would undermine the great spiritual achievements of human culture. Nor are these suggestions intended to bring into question or belittle the play techniques, "maturation devices," and other procedures developed within the past fifty or seventy-five years for early childhood education, beginning with the once revolutionary kindergarten. In terms of this analysis the latter are clearly "sensational" forms; but it must be noted that the first human expressions of all, when mankind was completely in the dark about the nature of his environment and his own role in relation to it, were the naturalistic, sensational images that survive in the primitive cave paintings of southwestern Europe and North Africa. Although analytical expression precedes the sensational stage of any given culture, an awed and groping sensationalism came first of all in paleolithic art (Plate 1a).

Childhood is a period dominated by the functions of consuming to a greater degree during the early stages than is ever again possible except in extreme illness and old age. The human infant must undergo an extensive period of familiarizing himself with the complex natural and social environment into which he has been born, before he can undertake the most elementary steps toward logical understanding. Grammar cannot be taught a child until he has been speaking fluently for many years, yet it is generally the basis of instruction in a new language for an adult.

Obviously a child is simply a consumer getting what he needs by demand of various sorts based on a paradoxical exercise of power within the family circle, and expressing himself in play activity. A complete exposition of an educational philosophy cannot be undertaken here, but the dynamics of a human personality changing from an infant consumer to an adult producer, and then to a sophisticated adult consumer in varying degrees, certainly must have some bearing. At present there are more serious confusions between stages one and three than meet the eye, due to excessive suppression of stage two, which is relegated largely to the vocational area.

Insofar as a child's play is related to life, it is imitative of the superficial patterns it has observed, just as a child's paintings present chiefly his reaction to appearances with no analytical correspondence in respect to scale, structure or other practical considerations. Bright colors, gay sounds, motion, novelty and fantasy attract the child's attention, and sweets are always welcome. Patterns of orderly living can be induced in the child at first only by patient training as with any other animal, rather than by appeal to reason. Any suggestions of logic must initially present only the broadest and simplest relations, rather as an introduction to the process than with any insistence on its reliability as a technique. Many of the practical results that some children seem to achieve are accomplished actually by performing what is to them an effective ritual rather than a creative process of cause and effect. However, the change in attitude goes on apace, and it can sometimes be marvelously accelerated by bringing the youth into contact with gradually more complex experience susceptible of analytical clarification, provided it remains always within his grasp.

Personal fulfillment in any given society lies in achieving standards of conduct which are to a degree sensational, being concerned with aesthetic and emotional sophistication, developed as more elementary aspects of objective practical reference become established and taken for granted. A serious educational pitfall, however, may be encountered in attempting to teach a child the sophisticated forms without contact with the process whereby they were developed out of an earlier, more practical, analytical stage. Several evils result. One is a stereotyped lifelessness in patterns of social elegance and morality, which seem empty and unconvincing to the rising generation. Any validity such standardized forms may have will apply only to the life of a single group in society, which the others are forced blindly to emulate. Much of the immaturity of contemporary "American" culture is due to a partly justified but negative revolt against this sort of artificiality.

Some educators under pressure of children's resistance to logical emphasis, have tried prolonging the primitive infantile stage of consumer. Play techniques and "projects" which merely mimic productive adult activity may be used excessively on the basis that experience is organic and not synthetic, that it is indivisible and destroyed in the process of analysis, etc. To be sure, the introduction of *abstract* logic at too early a stage, unwarranted speed in deriving practice from principle, is disastrous; but past failures due to such bad practice must not be permitted to discredit the analytical approach entirely.

When carried to extreme, elision of the analytical, logical factor from the educational process yields a personality deformed by partial retardation. Without practical orientation to the material world, or responsible orientation to the social and economic world, the first work situation, or other serious involvement in adult life, causes a rude awakening, often accompanied by serious setbacks. This is the cause of the widespread complaint that "I learned nothing in school." Those who are situated well enough to escape such painfully tardy discipline are not better off, but worse. For they move into the stage of adult consumer burdened with an unresolved residue of childhood. Familiar symptoms include unrealistically self-centered emotional demands, asserted in excessively importunate terms. However much an individual may achieve satisfactions by such means, he is bound to suffer some frustrations, which will seem devastatingly more threatening and painful than they would to a more practical person.

The dual objective of the educational process is clear. An infant consumer must be introduced gradually to the notion of logical sequence, and induced to abandon impulsive, sensational techniques of reacting to environment in favor of clearly reliable procedures logically adapting means to ends. When the forms and aims of his particular society are thus analytically understood, more recondite patterns of sophistication may be disclosed to a young adult, who will *then* be in a position to exploit them creatively for the true glory of a Golden Age, rather than to produce imitatively the artificialities of an eclectic or provincial situation.

# 6

# Subject Matter as an Aspect of Style

STYLE IS THE EFFECT PRODUCED BY THE EXPRESSIVE ASPECTS OF FORM IN art regardless of any natural reference or subject matter that may be involved. But an important stylistic factor is the *relation* of form to subject matter. Art is essentially the expression of an intensely desired goal, the celebration of vastly important successes, the statement of human purpose couched in highly organized sensuous terms to attract, hold, and intensify human attention. Anything that can be said in a work of art can be said more exactly, more completely in the verbiage of law, philosophy, science; but who besides professionals would be moved to action? The delights of color, light, movement, sound might be composed more ecstatically had they nothing to say; but then they could never become the focus of human attention, and must remain ever the periphery. Both must always be present in a major work of art. One bends to accommodate the other, and there is a pattern in this accommodation that constitutes an expressive element of style.

The degree to which an artist suppresses either the objective reference or the sensuous appeal, the ratio in which sense and description are blended, follow a pattern and carry a meaning referable to the analytical and sensational poles. Obviously a style concerned with giving an adequate picture of the material presented would relate to the clarifying tendencies of the analytical category; one with objective reference minimized in favor of emphasis on the aesthetic qualities of the composition would correspond to the obscurity of structure and exposition pertinent to the sensational category. Realistic art expresses the personalities of those who have intense practical concern, and predominates in early, creative stages. Styles where distortion is admitted for aesthetic effect or where description of shapes is allowed to dissolve as in chiaroscuro or the imprecise clouds of exciting color notes used by the impressionists, express a lack of practical orientation which marks the consumer attitude characteristic of late periods, supported by luxurious, strongly entrenched patronage.

A special effort must be made in assessing the degree of its reality, to realize that a work which *looks* most convincingly like some familiar scene may not be the most profoundly realistic presentation possible. Optic realization of form has already been seen to convey a less practical concern than tactile realization, and it is also true that an artist can analyze many aspects of subject matter to give a more profound exposition of some phase of life than could be gained by the most careful counterfeit of any actual scene or situation. It may be difficult to see the highly particularized genre painting of the seventeenth century, for example, especially in Holland, as falling short of the most perfectly realistic achievement (Plate 39). Of course, as the production of the first free bourgeois nation, these works must indeed express a vast concern with the objective material world. But the artists of the Low Countries had been quite skillfully exhibiting such concern in the plastic arts for patrons who had been citizens of free towns for centuries. Such continuity brought about advanced optic refinement of style, and the subjects chosen represent for the most part a rather light-hearted and effortless life of individual personal concern, not the commerce and manufacture that actually made Holland great. Almost all of Vermeer's paintings and those of de Hooch are concerned with the leisurely activities of a few people. Scenes of peasants at this time generally show them carousing in inns or family parties rather than at work in the fields, as Breughel so often painted them in the previous century. To be sure, Vermeer repeatedly shows a map on the back wall of his quiet interiors, indicating a contemporary concern with maritime trade, and a group of minor specialists devoted themselves to marine subjects, but with little practical exposition.

Wölfflin points out an interesting contrast between Leonardo's *Last Supper,* in which all twenty-six hands are visible (Plate 5a), and Rembrandt's much later *Syndics of the Cloth Guild* where a group of men is again composed behind a table, but only five hands out of twelve remain in view (Plate 39b). Rembrandt's group portrait is of course quite realistic in an optic sense, but this willingness to show things as they appear rather than as they are, begins a turning away from penetrating exploration of the real world toward a more cursory sensation of particular aspects, which ends in complete aesthetic emphasis and abstraction. This change in attitude toward subject matter is brought about by exactly the same apractical and self-indulgent social objectives as bring about concern with the sensational aspects of form.

Between the still highly realistic, though optic, treatment of form employed by Rembrandt and twentieth century abstraction or non-objectivism, there is obviously a considerable range of attitude, although they all correspond in general to the sensational category of style. Also the term "realism," defined as an interest in the objective content of a work of art, may be applied to a variety of expressions and in comparative degrees. The question, "How is reality expressed?" may be answered fairly simply. It is done either by analytical and tactile means, expressing a highly practical approach, or by sensational and optic means, expressing a less practical approach. But the question, *"What* reality is expressed?" requires an answer which may be equally if not more revealing, in relation to which the distinction previously made between the interests of producer and consumer has paramount significance.

Nero's notorious "fiddling" while Rome burned is an extreme example of the persistence or priority of personal interests in the face of events of overshadowing importance to the community. Similarly egocentric emphasis in varying degrees characterizes the treatment of subject matter in late stages of cultural development. Thus, however realistically the material *within the frame* of a picture may be presented, as in the work of the "boulevard realists" of the nineteenth century— Degas, Toulouse-Lautrec, Manet—the result may be only relatively realistic as a complete expression of the period, in view of what is *left out* of the frame. Mechanized industry and transportation were two of the greatest revolutions in the way of life that took place in the nineteenth century, yet what treatment do they encounter in the fine arts? Almost none. Monet did a few paintings like the *Old St. Lazare Station* (Plate 40b), which recognizes the *presence* of the railroad, the *pictorial* contribution it makes to the Parisian scene, but there is nothing connecting it with human life in the way that Daumier's *Third Class Carriage* does for example, or several of his paintings of people waiting in a railroad station, whose faces express various types of absorption in the adventure of their journey (Plate 40a). Turner's *Rain, Steam and Speed* (Plate 10b) is even more completely aestheticized than the Monet. With few exceptions a straightforward exposition of this important basic development can only be found in the popular art form of color lithography, like the Currier and Ives prints (Plate 10a).

Obviously therefore, mere recognizability of the objects presented is not an adequate criterion of practical realism expressing the analytical taste of the producer. Highly sensational style, however faithfully it appears to follow a particular subject, may lack profoundly realistic intent in two ways. First, it may present a thoroughly optic impression accentuating accidents of lighting and perspective to convey a minimum tactile realization of the forms. Second, the scope of a particularized subject may be so fragmentary and inconsequential, the interest so romantic, that it is actually unrealistic or misleading in terms of any broad view. To be sure a particular subject may be skillfully selected to imply a vast range of human feelings or operations. A Dutch interior by Vermeer (Plate 39a) or deHooch implies certain bourgeois aims of domestic leisure and material substance, but there is very little reference to the means whereby they are achieved.

It is frequently suggested that any such exposition of actuality is undesirable, the function of art being to "get away from the same old thing," and to let the imagination "soar above" ordinary life, which thereby seems to be rated categorically boring or repulsive. Obviously this is less a valid generalization than a confession. It reveals the curious paradox that, though the art of the consumer is most assertive of personal individuality, there is little or no genuine pride in the role itself; whereas a producer feels the undeniable though limited social status and identification based on his productive activity, however restricted its scope may be. The distinctly American saying about the "better mousetrap" was far more significant culturally as an expression of this sort of practical self-confidence than of an economic truth that indeed is already out of date.

Pioneer conditions in American life have inspired much practical orientation in its cultural expression. In the early history of the United States, for example, processions to honor important personages and events were made up largely of tradesmen in working garb, accompanied by floats presenting the activities and products of their respective trades. County fairs have played an important role in the social activity of the agricultural hinterland. They may have had their Midways, but the main purpose was the exhibition and acknowledgement of superior production; and the response of a farmer to a fine melon or high-bred Holstein raised by his neighbor is not a mere technical awareness or economic concern, but a genuine emotional excitement as well, with all the humanistic implications of the early Olympiads (Plate 47b).

In literature, photography and the cinema there has been a considerable development of "documentary" expression, and there is also extensive practice of the crafts in America for leisure-time occupation by people who make their livings in other ways. Both clearly indicate a cultural interest in objective, realistic expression not found proportionately in the plastic arts. On the contrary, critics in America are quite proud of this country's advancement of sophistication in the fine arts by so-called "action painting" (Motherwell, Kline, et al.) and other extreme, nonobjective expressions (Plate 44b). Interest in such trends predominates throughout the "official art world" of museums, galleries and publications concerned with their activities. It must be noted, however, that all this ultrasophistication touches only a minute portion of the population, even of those culturally and economically qualified to constitute a market for more meaningful expression, who need some legible human reference in the arts.

### ABSTRACTION: DISINTEREST OR CRITICAL REVOLT?

Though boredom, guilt, or fear in the minds of an economically independent elite doubtless account for many phases of latter-day European culture, another more constructive motivation has been claimed for distortion and abstraction in twentieth-century art, and in fact has been commonly cited by the artists themselves, especially in the group manifestoes with which many of the new styles were launched. Their mocking, nihilistic rejection of the world around them is attributed in these documents to a revolutionary antagonism to the political and social ills of industrial society, freely admitted among some of the circles that profited most from it. Disregarding the obscurity of their communication for the general public, they insisted that their critical attitude was a progressive and objective concern. Is it therefore stylistically analytical in terms of the present analysis, as it would be if it were indeed the expression of a new way of life?

Two considerations of paramount importance must be brought to the determination of whether early twentieth-century art is actually the end of the old or the beginning of the new. One is the question as to which is more truly significant for the interpretation of society through art: the personality of the artist and his motives in creating a particular style, or those of his patrons in supporting it? Any possible difference between the personal attitudes of artist and patron would tend to be most marked in a late stage, when the artist must express the attitude of the consumer, although serious application to his work (whether pursued for economic necessity or not) makes him something of a producer who must often cultivate a high degree of technical skill. Therefore, though he must understand, he cannot identify fully with the whimsical rejection of practical concern that he must express for a society of consumers. In such periods he may even capitalize on the display of certain practical aspects of his craft as an elaborate mystery, like the academician who frequently squints at the landscape past his thumb held at arm's length, or who must pepper his conversation on art with quasi-technical words in foreign languages. Insofar as he may be conscious of any considerable difference in attitude from that of his patrons, he may even include concealed or playful criticism of them in his work, as the court jester proverbially rallied the king. The entire Dada movement was of course essentially satirical (Plate 45), and much of the content of Picasso's later work lampoons many of those who innocently admire it. However, when these artists enjoyed commercial success, the acceptance of their work was based on its bizarre, i.e., sensational, character that was manifest to the collector and the public, not on any quasi-analytical criticism that was largely privy to the artist and his intimate circle.

The other question to be considered in interpreting the complex objectives of twentieth-century art is whether negative criticism of an old society actually identifies its muckrakers and Cassandras as the initiators of a new order and stylistic cycle, or is merely the lament of the disinherited. For an analytical expression is motivated characteristically by the establishment and celebration of new sources of human fulfillment. Giotto does not ridicule Byzantine style, but merely tries to improve upon it. When David criticizes the corruption of the body politic in his early classical paintings, like the *Oath of the Horatii* or the *Death of Socrates* (Plate 38a), he does so by extolling the virtues he anticipates in the new order. In any transition the gains of the new order coexist for a considerable period with the evils of the old. The creative, constructive responsibility of the artist who chooses to identify himself with progress is to distinguish and demonstrate the nature and superiorities of the new order so that its nascent characteristics may be clearly seen and fostered despite the lingering glamor of the no longer valid culture that is passing.

### GENERAL VS. SPECIFIC REFERENCE

Within the field of naturalistic expression there are also two attitudes that fit perfectly with the polar categories. Truth has its generalized and specific aspects, already touched upon to some extent. Generalized description (when it is not evasively vague, of course) is analytical and practical because it requires logical correlation of a number of observations to arrive at a constant essence. It results in elimination of accidental variations, leaving a dependable, operative principle that is serviceable for future use. Emphasis of specific aspects of reality is of less practical value, because an isolated phase or appearance might never be encountered again. To remark it in art is capricious, although in science it might be useful as a clue to a hitherto undiscovered generality. Concern with the specific implies a late stage of a particular cultural evolution, because it takes the generalization for granted, otherwise its accidental aspects would be confusing rather than entertaining. It implies the self-centered role of the consumer, who has no use for practical information; and prefers to notice the specific, unusual aspects of form, for to do so is to express the uniqueness of a particular person's experience, personality or observation.

There is also a middle ground, namely, specific reference that is nevertheless typical. Many of the landscapes of Breughel or the nautical paintings and Adirondack scenes of Winslow Homer are quite convincing in their documentary detail (Plate 47a), yet it is obvious in each that the artist refers to a general type of activity, behind which is the deeper notion of man's heroism or resourcefulness when confronted with raw natural force. This is somewhat different from the mere reportage of a newspaper photo of floods in the Middle West, which might be captioned,

"Mrs. Hepzibah MacLevy, aged 83, of Fourth River Avenue, Four Rivers, Mo., is helped from a second-story window of her home after a night of sleepless terror with her pet cormorant and Weimaraner, by Corporal A. B. Canotier of the local Civil Defense forces. (ZP Photo from Wide-Wide News Service.)"

An excellent illustration of how a realistic presentation in art may be given a generalized treatment appears in the contrast between early and late landscape painting. The landscapes of Poussin (Plate 27a) and Claude, early Turners of his "classical" period, early Inness, in the broad inclusive sweep and variety of their material—trees, streams, hills, a town, some ruins, cattle, farmhouses—seem to be a catalogue, a summary, a *general* statement of what a natural scene comprises. Paintings of the Barbizon school, late Turner, late Inness, on the other hand, present a specific place, a single tree, a farmhouse, a woodland stream, a few animals in a field, even the effect of light at a particular time of a particular kind of day.

When Breughel decided to paint a picture of children at play, he did not stop with two or three. He painted a picture with dozens of children playing every kind of game he could think of. If an artist were interested in the theater and wished to make a painting of it, he might study how to combine a representation of the audience seated attentively in a dark house, the actors performing on a brightly lit stage, an orchestra in between, and perhaps a glimpse of the mechanics of production through the wings. Such a presentation was never attempted by Degas, one of the foremost painters of the theater in the late nineteenth century. For him, intimacy was reality, and he showed an actual performance only as he may have seen it obliquely from the wings; in fact, he seemed to prefer the even more fragmentary and intimate approach of painting rehearsals.

Generalization being analytical is found in early cultural stages. Not before the seventeenth century could an artist paint *a* mother and child; it had to be *The Mother and Child*. But by the fifteenth century it could at least *look like* a specific mother and child, as in some of the Madonnas of Fra Filippo Lippi. The change from one extreme to another was accomplished, as is so frequently the case, in several stages.

A specific subject may be so pertinent and widely known as to have a general implication, like David's *Death of Marat* or his *Tennis Court Oath*, which represent different types of service and heroism in the cause of the French Revolution. Enough reportorial detail is included in each case to establish the actuality of the incident, but not to interfere with a realization of its outstanding importance. Events of this sort may achieve a quasi-symbolical character, and, if they are widely enough accepted to be frequently recalled, actually become a symbol of the quality or meaning that gives the subject its general importance.

SYMBOLISM

Symbolism is a type of generalization in which the reduction of reality or detail is so complete and the allusion so deeply motivated that a critical determination has to be made in each case as to whether the expression is truly realistic and analytical or not. Thus the personification of natural forces in Greek mythology was for that stage of society a humanistic attempt to present the realities of natural environment, at least as they affect the life of man, and can be considered thoroughly analytical. The Greek gods may be depicted in a mural painting or sculptured monument today, however, precisely for the purpose of evading any significant assertion about the nature of reality (Plate 46a), as indicated above in the discussion of eclecticism. Thus a symbolical device, presented in an academically imitated linear style, may appear confusingly in what is obviously a period predominantly expressing the interests of the consumer.

Medieval morality plays, in which human qualities were personified, represented the first step in trying to realize human personality on the modern stage, and were obvious symbolic generalizations, as realistic for their time as the more particular type of realism that predominates in the theater today. Saints depicted with the instruments of their martyrdom were symbols of salvation throughout the early Middle Ages, and since salvation was then a force of universal reality in human motivation, they may be considered realistic within their historical frame of reference. As this reality lapsed, artists began to invest their saints with a more specific, narrative reality, using incidents from their lives which were presented as intimate domestic scenes. Still later, as literal belief in the Scriptural narrative came to be considered naïve, these subjects were again formulated, but in a manner embodying physical and emotional appeal, which carries a conviction of reality only for the faithful. Many aspects of modern culture are handled in a similarly ingratiating fashion, so that the term "generalization" frequently associated with the adjective "vague," is often applied to a process of evading real issues as well as to serious, constructive assertion of basic principles in the sense used here.

Symbols that are widely accepted or readily recognizable are a means of clarifying or evoking reality, at least in its broader aspects, most suitable for periods of relatively uncomplicated cultural unanimity. Considerable confusion results from the practice in art criticism of applying the term also to forms and objects that happen to represent an important aspect of life to a particular individual, like the subconscious sexual reference certain shapes may have. For example, frequent reference to "the mountains of Nebraska" was supposed to reveal the gradual involvement of a young clergyman with a lady of easy virtue in the play *Rain*, produced many years ago. Willem deKooning's paintings of women (Plate 46b) have a symbolic quality. The recurrent bull in Picasso's work is frequently thought to represent political brutality, as in the mural symbolizing the destruction of Guernica; but his other bulls are less ferocious and a number of explanations have been offered regarding the meaning of Picasso's bull. Symbols of this type may be more or less accessible to sophisticated beholders in view of the increasing currency of knowledge about subconscious processes of the human mind. The determination as to whether or not, and how much, they contribute to the analytical and clarifying force of the style in a particular work, can only be made in terms of how readily the symbols are understood and how widely they are adopted. If the impreciseness of the symbol simply provides an intriguing subject for speculation, or stimulates inconclusively a broad area of feeling (as an ameba-like shape of Miro might do (Plate 45b), or even the "emergent forms" of Salvador Dali) it becomes a matter of personal entertainment, obviously a consumer value.

To add a new symbol to the cultural vocabulary of any people is a profoundly creative intuitive accomplishment, but the process of its recognition must have some kind of immediacy as the term is used here. To take an unclear painting based on unrecognizable aesthetic elements, and speculatively attach Freudian or other subconscious meanings to the shapes involved as "symbols" of the artist's profound reaction to some aspect of life, is to use the word in a way that does not indicate any widely legible expression of reality. The work may well have a greatness of its own, and a rich appeal to the beholder who has the equipment and inclination to get involved in it, and for whom the challenging subtlety of invention may indeed be a great attraction. The esoteric inaccessibility of such values is akin to those suggested for the sensational category of form, in the nature of entertainment rather than exposition. They express a late stage of cultural development and have only a limited popular appeal.

## SOPHISTICATED ADMIRATION OF PRIMITIVE ART

Abstraction and distortion have characterized both primitive and sophisticated cultures. Artists functioning without any practical concern in European society of the early twentieth century actually adopted and imitated the relatively abstract forms of African Negro sculpture. Does this common interest in the same type of form by two so vastly different societies argue against the social expression of style? Or does it reveal significant subconscious parallels in the attitudes of both societies to their respective environments?

As indicated in the previous discussion, the geometrical designs, structural modifications and inverted ratios of natural proportion in primitive art, like that of central Africa and Oceania, represent a tentative assertion of human superiority over nature, with some fearful or wishful religio-magic purpose. An element of human logic, however simple, is involved in these various devices, for the regularity of geometrical design (which originated from a special delight in the regular pattern of the craftsman's strokes, as discussed above, p. 122) is the human opposite of the complex disorder found in nature. Geometrical simplifications of parts of the body or other natural objects into cones, cylinders and spheroids is again a humanistic assertion, for simple geometrical shapes are rare in nature.

This urgency of human assertion is brought about by the conditions of living in a primitive economy dependent on the uncertain bounties of natural supply, and subject to the hazards of natural catastrophe. Nature is a Leviathan that primitive man must try to ride. It provides food and shelter, but their occurrence seems to be an accident and a mystery, however manageable this becomes in neolithic times. A tension bordering on enmity toward natural environment arises in the human mind. The hunting tribes at first showed no consciousness of self in the realistic cave drawings, concerned chiefly with the intended quarry; man still conceived himself a natural creature not at all distinct from his environment. Natural representation was the mystical, awesome need of the nomadic hunting society and it was skillfully accomplished in cave paintings throughout southern Europe and North Africa perhaps 25,000 years ago. But with the advent of settled communities and agriculture, resulting in some sense of man's potential control of nature, the human race dared to feel a quasi-antagonistic distinctness from the rest of the natural universe, which was expressed by abandoning objectives of completely realistic representation. The vocabulary of geometric devices or modifications of natural form which the neolithic artists proceeded to derive from patterns, shapes and motions of craft manufacture, served exactly to express the new sense of independence.

It was a similar assertion of distinctness from or rejection of environmental forces that caused the aesthetically hypersophisticated European in the early nineteen hundreds to accept African sculpture. Throughout the nineteenth century, people involved in colonial government and trade had occasionally brought back such objects as personal souvenirs or anthropological curiosities (Plate 13b, 43a). They were hardly considered objects of art at all, but in the decade before World War I, important collections were made by a few prominent connoisseurs of art. Obvious stylistic imitation followed, as in Picasso's period of *Les Demoiselles d'Avignon* (Plate 42) and Modigliani's style generally, in the sculpture of Brancusi, and the work of many later artists (Plate 43b).

What expressive force can this strange material retain for the twentieth century? Natural environment, to be sure, is well under control; so well, so completely that the city dweller considers the flow of natural produce to his kitchen or dining table to be virtually automatic. For the rentier, who is the chief patron of art in this society, the physical necessities of life just happen. Of course he has heard something of the existence of an industrial system and organized agriculture, but there is little about them that he can understand in terms of his own personality, which is in fact revolted by almost any aspect of the work-a-day world he happens to encounter. Extensive systemization; regular, scheduled application to a repetitive task set by the need for highly detailed coordination with the operations of other people; self-discipline and a considerable period of personal submergence in a secondary role in order to master skills, manual or intellectual; all of which are of the essence of industrial production at the basis of human existence today, inflict on some people a sense of claustrophobia, frustration and even personal disfigurement.

This tension and antagonism toward the basically necessary productive environment brings about invention of cultural artificialities to make life tolerable. The offensive image of the strange new *social* Leviathan, into which world-wide integration of industrial production and trade has welded the vast majority of the population, must be submerged. To this end it becomes quite appropriate, especially in a period of rampant eclecticism, and when the poor artists' heads are splitting over the increasing tempo of demands for novelty, to borrow a formula of artificiality that had been used by mankind at the dawn of human culture to exorcise the poorly understood, threatening enormities of the *natural* Leviathan.

Reference to the chief period in which European culture had previously rejected the appearances of reality in art shows clearly similar motivation. Distortion and abstraction in the elaborately interlaced patterns of Hiberno-Saxon manuscript illumination (Plate 20), the angular contours of saints and the nervously scrawling line of some of the Carolingian styles, were used in the early Middle Ages when violence and poverty had made earthly environment well-nigh intolerable, the pattern of life highly haphazard, and human attention was concentrated on the hope of heavenly glory with the frenzied intensity of a panic retreat from reality.

### ALTERNATIVES OF SUBJECT MATTER

The selection and treatment of subject matter may be seen from the foregoing discussion to present two pairs of alternatives, which should be considered in any stylistic analysis of a work of art. First, the artist may choose to turn toward or away from the world of objective reality, of things as they are or seem to be. No art worthy of any distinction, of course, is a complete or mechanical repetition of appearances; some clarification if only by reduction and control of the total material detail must be imposed by the artist, and sensuous or formal elements may be added to achieve artistic significance.

The artist who chooses to turn *toward* the world of objective reality, and to assert his own creative personality without interfering with the impression of undistorted verisimilitude, has nevertheless an extensive range. He may, according to the expressive requirements of his society, take any suitable position between the extremes of a highly generalized clarification of his subject material, and a particular, even momentary reportage or appreciation of what he has chosen to portray. That is to say, he may choose to exploit the commonality of experience that is inherent in the subject he has selected, for the elucidation of all men; or he may present the special flavor of experience derived from the impact on his own personality of some particular thing he has encountered and selected for the enjoyment of those who are sympathetic to his own orientation.

The artist who chooses to turn *away* from objective reality, who will make something based completely on inner motivation, using reference to real objects and occurrences only as they happen to arise in his purely subjective vision, distorted or juxtaposed so that no actual circumstance could possibly seem to be intended, also has two alternatives. The forms and sensations he employs may be directed either to emotional or aesthetic effects. That is to say, he may make a concrete reference to the external world, but in highly personal, virtually subconscious terms; or, on the other hand, manipulation of aesthetic elements (as in a piece of instrumental music) may be the artist's entire apparent concern, let the emotional connotations be what they may, or arise from whatever mood he may happen to be in.

These latter alternatives are not at all exclusive of one another. A nostalgic dream picture of his native peasant village by Chagall (Plate 44a) may be presented in colors that are sensuously exciting as well as suggestive of an appropriate mood. Likewise in a completely nonobjective work the forms may admit of some more or less obvious emotional interpretation based on rhythm, tempo, key of tone or color, and so on.

Together these alternatives present a master scale of attitudes toward subject matter from analysis to sensation, motivated as in the categories of form by the general cultural attitude of the artist and the society of which he is a part. At one extreme is objective material presented in terms of a clear, generalized reality, followed by objective material presented more selectively according to particular individual preferences. Next is subjective material with a principally emotional reference, and, at the opposite extreme from generalized reality, is completely nonobjective creation, synthesized from abstract aesthetic elements. One end of the scale represents complete extroversion or social identification; the other represents extreme introversion, a social independence and emphasis on personal distinctions, which is virtually antagonistic to a vast portion of mankind, and resentful of any suggestion of social interdependence.

Confusion has arisen lately insofar as some artists and critics have insisted that there is a superior reality in the subjective choice and handling of subject matter, in view of the tremendous force lately recognized in subconscious motivation of human life. It must be borne in mind, however, that the motivations of realistic art, despite the fact that they are widely legible, also arise from sources deeply imbedded in human personality. Interest in one's neighbor, participation in the surrounding community, delight in the common wonders of the material universe, are derived as much from emotional aspects of personality as is any impulse to introspection and social aloofness or idiosyncrasy. Eccentricity does not represent *more* personality, but simply a certain kind. The categorically revolutionary quality of genius *seems* to be supported by the need vital personalities have felt at times in the past, to reject stultifying conventions imposed by narrow social groups. In such cases it might be said, however, that *the society itself* must be judged eccentric in relation to basic natural impulses of human personality, and dissent considered a sign of true or larger social identification.

# 7

# Conclusion and Epilogue

THE PROBLEM NATURAL SCIENTISTS HAD TO SOLVE BEFORE FURTHER progress could be made was that of analyzing matter. Chemistry could do little before establishing the basic elements of which all substances are composed. Biology is greatly indebted to the microscope that makes possible a study of cellular structure, and to analytical techniques like anatomy. Physics has been concerned in considerable degree with the granular or cellular, then molecular, and now atomic structure of matter. In the presence of any given substance or object, the natural scientist attacks his problem by asking, "Of what is it composed?"

In the social sciences, among which the history and appreciation of art belong, the field of observation is already atomized. All about are people, human deeds and social events. The problem is to find the significant patterns into which they fit. The social scientist stares at his cells, his atoms and molecules, day in and day out; they are everywhere about him, constantly, but what is the body they compose? Some little clusters are obvious: the family, age groups, political units, income levels; but over long periods of time, whole social systems, the entire perspective of man's life on earth, what are the significantly inclusive patterns? Where is the instrument that will allow the student of individual and social personality to examine their growth from the beginning? He can stop any one of the contemporary cells on the street and inquire about his feelings, activities and associations. The technique of the "market survey" is quite advanced, and Univac may readily process the gatherings; but this is only a step toward digesting such material into operative basic intuitions, and can be applied only to the living. What form of fossilized record or impacted strata of human experience have the others left from ages past? Where is the *macroscope* with which the developing totality can be viewed?

The history of cultural expression can be most serviceable in this illuminating role. The plastic arts have a more extensive and complete history than any other, possibly excepting literature, which lacks contact with the vast prehistoric life of man and is veiled by differences of language. First, of course, the role of art in human society must be correctly understood: *Art is human experience aesthetically enhanced and organically perfected for expansion of the scope of human attention.* Present concepts of art as escape, fantasy, play, sensuous and intellectual titillation, must be read not as a description of art, but of the pattern of experience idealized by the limited group in contemporary society for whom so much of present-day painting and sculpture is created.

Next it is necessary to understand the complex path the human message must take in its transformation into a physical object (or performance, as in drama, dance and music) in order to discharge some localized function, spiritual or otherwise, as well as into a sensuous pattern to attract and penetrate human attention. Often the formal characteristics or *style* of the particular artistic creation may be clearer and more legible than its content or its objective reference. The latter may be highly diversified or almost nil, as in neolithic and early medieval styles, and in a great deal of modern art.

Clearly, then, the most important or most immediate requirement for the use of art as a macroscope in the social sciences is a proper understanding of the meaning of style. What are the motivations and dynamic of this process whereby social personality is impressed on the forms of artistic creation? It is a safe venture that never, throughout the earlier history of art when formal elements seemed to evolve with such inevitability and spontaneous acceptance, were artists as conscious of style as they are today, when it is nevertheless approached with utter confusion. The Renaissance gave Western Europe a Pandora's box of stylistic self-consciousness in its return to the classic. Then the Neo-classicists lifted the lid and let out the pestilential swarm of eclectic imitations to plague the arts with confused and superficial controversy. The distracting buzz can be dispelled now, only by going into the subject of style to clear up what it really is, as Pandora had at last to reopen the chest to let out the good fairy, Hope.

Unfortunately, for many people the word "style" has acquired the connotation of whimsical, superficial preferences like the annual gyrations in the fashion of women's clothing or new car models from Detroit. In art, however, style actually summarizes much that is deeply significant about a person or a society. Vital human personality is purposeful, decided on its objectives and the means of their achievement, which it seeks resolutely, not in ignorance of, but despite the complexity of environment and the unsolved mysteries of life. What else is maturity but just such an ability to decide, at the moment of action, what action is necessary? The broader and more flexible the purposes and patterns, the better the chances of success, but at any given moment the responsible adult personality must be able, ready or not, to decide what is to be done next, not in the frenzied fashion of constant improvisation, but in respect of some vitally important general direction, with sufficient self-assurance for effective performance.

Those who can muster this faith, vision, self-confidence, make their decisions at a deep level of personality that is served but not governed by intellect, and their lives have a clear, consistent and readable character. This deep governing pattern, subconscious character or emotional conviction informs the gestures of men in personal conduct and it is called "manners"; it guides the deeds of leaders in public life and it is called "ideals," "faith," or simply "judgment." It likewise informs the creations of artists. Then it is called "style," and through that style can be read the manners, ideals, faith and patterns of decision followed by the artist and the society for which the artist created, in its general attitudes toward life.

The artist who is the product of a society cooperating for its general advancement will have a socially oriented self-confidence, a feeling of "belonging," that is the essence of the finest humanism. Faith in his own powers as a man follows, inspiring achievements based on logical analysis and the discovery and use of order in his environment. This in turn produces an analytical philosophy and creative practice with the resultant stylistic characteristics detailed above as of the first category.

On the other hand, an artist identified with a group that is condescending or antagonistic to the society of which it is a part, subsisting on wealth appropriated by force or privilege, will view the world egotistically with a mystic or unconcerned attitude toward hows and whys, while the intuitive direction and virtuosity of his creative processes will emphasize sensation, fantasy, capricious or accidental effects pertaining to the sensational category of stylistic characteristics. In primitive cultures, mysticism and distortion may also express mankind's fearful antagonism toward physical environment.

Order and accident, logic and sensation, analysis and intuition, production and consumption, humanism as against mysticism or egotism, are all simply opposite extremes of human interest and behavior which seem to cluster about two poles of human personality. Style in cultural expression is a recording point or scriber that marks a line wavering between them on a moving time-graph as in a seismograph or a device for recording meteorological observations. It sums up the meaning, records the dominant attitude, and presents a macroscopic perspective of the multitude of historical, economic, and ethnological circumstances that may be operating at the indicated point.

The focusing power of the history of art as macroscope, in a manner referred to several times previously, presents certain exciting possibilities of philosophical pioneering. The instrument is actually so strong that it can draw the entire range of human culture into a single pattern, as artists sometimes inspect the broader aspects of a complex composition through the large end of a pair of binoculars. A hopeful prescription for achievement of the highest human aims may clearly be read in the observation that stylistic opposites tend to coalesce in the process of stylistic evolution, already pointed out in various connections (pp. 32, 103).

All of man's unceasing efforts to affect his natural and social environment have oscillated between two extremes. Some have over emphasized the necessity to reject or rise above the apparently impenetrable complexities of cosmic and human nature with logically constructed patterns and exclusions. Others underestimated the effectiveness of human ability to discover or establish orderliness of any appreciable scope. Through countless ages when these attitudes in isolation appeared antagonistic, an occasional burst of brilliance has reflected from a moment of interaction, which proves that the two opposite attitudes are not indeed incompatible.

Furthermore, it is clear that although an oscillatory, almost cyclical alternation of the two views characterizes the history of human culture, each swing is to a gradually less extreme position. The respective attitudes increasingly limit and qualify one another. However, up to the present, cultural growth has been quite subjective and accidental. The brilliant Golden Ages of full power were brought about entirely by passing historical coincidence, and could not be maintained beyond the briefest span.

The current Golden Age of the natural sciences reveals the possibility of consciously resolving antagonistic or alternative tendencies hitherto associated with the analytical—sensational polarity, thus extending perhaps indefinitely the periods of humanistic triumph. Since the intellectual Renaissance (or *Éclairecissement*) of such great minds as Galileo, Descartes, Newton (not a period, exactly, but a stage, for foretastes appear as far back as Abelard and Roger Bacon), scientific practice has been guided by strictly logical absolutes, such as the laws of motion or of the conservation of mass and energy. Yet this has in no way precluded the most minute and exhaustive submission of the scientific mind to the complexity of natural environment in an endless program of examination and experimentation. Formula and phenomenon must agree; neither may distort or ignore the other.

The result is a state of mind in which no problem appears categorically insoluble, however tortuous its solution may prove to be. Programs and techniques, however much they may require subsequent modification, are readily developed for the solution of any problem out of the terms of the problem itself. All such logical structures projected for scientific purposes take fully into account whatever degree of complexity may be presented by the objective phenomena involved, and are prepared to search methodically and with sustained confidence through an endless series of hypothetical possibilities.

Emotions and prejudices such as once blocked the road of the natural scientists still restrain the social scientists in respect to many of their prescriptions for control and amelioration of human society. Enough has been done, however, by way of solving certain age-old mysteries of human personality to show clearly that successes paralleling those of the natural sciences can be achieved when society is ready. The hopeful results to date have been accomplished by a combination of analytical and sensational inspiration which might be said to represent a relaxation of the analytical pattern and a submission to phenomenal subtleties in an even greater degree than is required by the natural sciences, without becoming utterly subjective. The greatest advance thus far has occurred in the understanding of individual personality. More serious obstacles are met when attempts are made to approach objectively the problems of social organization.

The Golden Age of social science will not introduce mankind to an earthly paradise or Nirvana in which no problems exist, nor would any sound mind in a sound body wish it so. The need for mankind to extract subsistence from his natural environment will continue, and since acquired characteristics are not transmitted, the entire process of social adjustment must be reconstituted within each new individual and generation. The limitations of human consciousness being what they are, a global society embracing nearly three billion individuals must continue to be constellated out of groupings that vary widely in scope and complexity; and the adjustments between them, however equable and intelligently arrived at, will also require endless consideration.

For these high aims, the fallacy that analytical and sensational approaches are incompatible must be enlightened in order to dispel the misunderstandings that have nurtured so much controversy among men. The techniques of antagonism are now so highly developed that their maintenance and effectiveness are on the verge of destroying life on earth. Much of the human race is ready to make the immediate sacrifices necessary to resolve the overpowering antagonisms, provided a formula can be discovered whereby the equability and effectiveness of such sacrifices may be assayed. The macroscope of cultural history cannot function as an electronic computer to produce such a formula. Its use is to scan the ebb and flow of human well-being in the past, which clearly indicates repeated successes from the interaction between analytical and sensational attitudes during the Golden Ages of so many different societies.

The present study cannot attempt to discern what forms such a coalition might produce in the field of the social sciences. The way is clearly indicated, however. Those who consider and plot the relations of men to one another must steer a resolute course between the Scylla of canonical prescriptions which may appear to have logical justification but are based actually on incomplete premises, and the Charybdis of subjective impulse emanating from finite personal leadership which cannot, without some analytical guidance, adequately identify itself with the broadest human interests. Such a resolution of the confusions of social philosophy may be expected to reveal guiding principles adequate to preserve life on earth from human violence, now its greatest hazard, as the scientific philosophers have been able to overcome the hazards that once threatened human survival from the recalcitrant and catastrophic forces of nature.

Perspectives of this sort may seem to lead far afield for those who regard the arts as pleasant entertainment. They are indeed offensive to that group for whom cultural activity is a means of screening off or denying aspects of reality that seem unpleasant or threatening to them. But for those who feel impelled to face the problems they see about them, and to seek first principles whereby they may be solved, the arts can serve as a valuable means of simplifying their appallingly complex outlines.

a. Paleolithic cave painting, Lascaux

b. Neolithic geometrical design. Large Zuni jar, New Mexico

The earliest men to leave any cultural record depended almost entirely on the hunt for survival. The consequent absorption in this crucial activity is shown by their mastery of lifelike images of the quarry. The precision and ryhthm of later geometrical design celebrates the elementary logic and craftmanship whereby the first agriculturists began to exert and feel some power over their environment.

PLATE 1

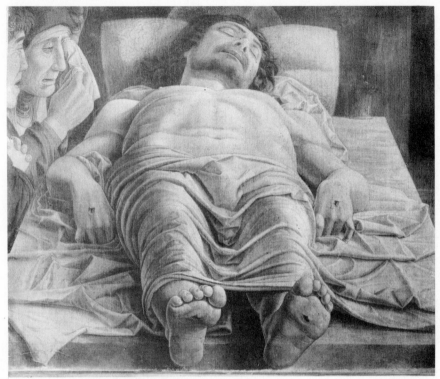

a. Andrea Mantegna (1431–1516). *Pietà*

It is not only the emotional treatment of the same subject that differs so strikingly in these paintings, done about two centuries apart in Italy. The quality of the forms is diametrically opposed and the differences are deeply and significantly motivated.

b. Annibale Caracci (1560–1609). *Pietà*

PLATE 2

a. Rembrandt van Rijn (1606–1669). *Study of a Nude Man.* Etching

b. Antonio Pollaiuolo (1429–1498). *Battle of the Ten Nudes.* Engraving

Although engraving and etching depend basically on a
line incised in a metal plate, the earlier artist shows
awareness of the possibility of fusing lines into tones.
But his work remains stylistically linear, while the later
artist produces a highly tonal effect.

PLATE 3

a. *Birth of Aphrodite*. Greek, 5th century B.C., low relief sculpture

In the early Greek Altar of Aphrodite, all of the forms
and their compositional movements conform to a narrow plane strictly parallel to the surface on which they
are developed. In the later structure they weave in and
out of the relief plane in a highly recessional pattern,
although in neither case is any spatial background
represented. (Compare Plate 33b)

b. *Battle of the Gods and Giants*. Hellenistic, high relief sculpture. Detail of
the Great Altar of Zeus.

PLATE 4

a. Leonardo da Vinci (1452–1519). *The Last Supper*. Church of S. Maria delle Grazie, Milan

b. Pieter Breughel the Elder (c. 1525–1569). *Peasant Wedding*

Both of these paintings are essentially analytical. Leonardo's mural seems more tonal than actually intended because his experiments with a new medium to replace fresco were not entirely successful and the work has deteriorated. Breughel's painting has a major recessional axis because of the northern tendency to accelerate sensational aspects of style, especially space.

PLATE 5

Giovanni Batista Tiepolo (1696–1770). *Banquet of Anthony and Cleopatra.*
Palazzo Labia, Venice

This is a perfectly flat wall merging through a simple cove
into a perfectly flat ceiling, except for the two doors and
two windows each surrounded on three sides by a narrow
marble frame. All the rest is painted in a manner which
discounts the limitations of enframement and picture plane
in order to effect a perfectly open composition.

PLATE 6

a. Edouard Manet (1832–1883). *Chez le Père Lathuille*

There is a kind of reality in the paintings of these "Boulevard realists," in their highly developed sense of unstaged, specific immediacy—in one, the young man's earnest expression, in the other, the seemingly accidental coincidence of the forms. But it is a reality pertaining strictly to the private lives of the individuals involved or the artist himself.

PLATE 7

b. Edgar Dégas (1834–1917). *At the Races*

National Gallery, Washington, D.C., Mellon Collection

The smallest detail in the earlier portrait clearly reveals what it represents, whereas several fairly large areas in the later portrait, like the hand or the sleeve sashes, are virtually meaningless except in relation to the whole.

a. Rogier van der Weyden (c. 1400–1464).
 *Portrait of a Lady*

Museo del Prado, Madrid (Anderson)

b. Diego Velásquez (1599–1660).
 *Portrait of the Artist,* detail from
 *The Maids of Honor.*

PLATE 8

a. The Parthenon, west facade, Athens. Greek, 5th century B.C.

(Alinari)

Everything in the design of the Parthenon refers aesthetically to the function of support and logical integration of parts. In the aristocratic Rococo palace, however, though the columns of a Greek order are used as the basis of its design, all sense of mass and support is discarded. Note the entablature broken out over the columns and the human figures used as supports for the elaborately decorated vaulting above.

b. Episcopal Palace, Würzburg Built 1720–1744. Architect: Balthasar Neumann

(German Tourist Information Office)

PLATE 9

a. Currier & Ives. *The "Lightning Express" Trains* (The Old Print Shop, New York)

b. J.M.W. Turner (1775–1851). *Rain, Steam and Speed*

Tate Gallery, London

Railroading was an exciting new development in the nineteenth century. Turner is concerned here only with the aesthetic spectacle it creates under certain atmospheric conditions. However, the artist employed by the publishing firm of Currier & Ives uncompromisingly presents, even in a night scene, the forms of locomotives and cars as well as many operating details which might easily be obscured in shadow. (Compare Plate 40)

PLATE 10

Despite his conscious concern with motion, Uccello was for technological as well as socioeconomic reasons an analytical artist. His insistent, tactile concentraion on form and structure therefore freezes the intended action according to a deeply motivated stylistic imperative, while Bernini gets a vastly greater sense of movement in a simple portrait.

a. Paolo Uccello (1397–1475). *Cavalry Battle,* detail of *Mounted Knights*

Uffizi Gallery, Florence (Alinari)

Royal Palace, Versailles (Giraudon)

b. Giovanni Lorenzo Bernini (1598–1680). *Portrait of Louis XIV, King of France*

PLATE 11

a. Vittore Carpaccio (1460–1522). Scenes from the series on the *Life of St. Ursula*

Three separate incidents of St. Ursula's life are spread across the picture plane of Carpaccio's entrancingly detailed harbor scene; whereas the form and concept of Tintoretto's "Presentation" are completely focussed on the central figure of a single event.

b. Iacopo Robusti Tintoretto (1518–1594). *Presentation of the Virgin* Church of the Madonna dell'Orto, Venice

PLATE 12

(Marburg)

a. Angel, detail of the *Last
Judgment*. Romanesque
period. Tympanum. Cathedral
of St. Lazare, Autun

Proportions of the human figure may be modified for various expressive purposes. The
Romanesque angel is attenuated in the intense,
antinatural spirit of early northern Christianity.
African sculptors distort the human figure, generally but not always *compressing* its ratios in
the neolithic spirit of asserting human power
over nature. This group also demonstrates the
use of proportion in showing the relative importance of the king and his attendants.

b. Group of figures from Benin, British Nigeria

PLATE 13

Museum für Volkerkunde (Walker Evans)

Michelangelo's sculpture is an excellent example of the power of a Golden Age or "transition of growth" to conserve the earlier sense of mass, as recessional movement and sensuous surface qualities are added. Giovanni da Bologna goes further toward the Baroque ideal of movement in space and sacrifices virtually all sense of bulk.

a. Michelangelo Buonarroti
(1475–1564). *Unfinished Slave*

b. Giovanni da Bologna (1524–1608).
*Mercury*

PLATE 14

Giovanni Lorenzo Bernini (1598–1680). *Tomb of Pope Alexander VII*. Church of St.
    Peter, Vatican, Rome

The relation of the figures to the enframing niche is the key to
an elaborate composition of complex movements, sensuous contrast of materials, actual and implied recessional circulation in
depth, and other Baroque characteristics, focussed in a single
dominant figure whose importance is thus celebrated.

PLATE 15

From spatially self-contained, analytically tactile delineation of form and structure as in the "Spearbearer," Greek sculptors go on to develop complex compositions radiating from a central focus, and often extensively involved with the immediate environment. Such is the case of "The Victory" alighting on the prow of a naval vessel which is erected at the edge of a reflecting pool.

Museum, Naples (Anderson)

a. Polykleitos *Spearbearer*. Greek, 5th century B.C.

Musée du Louvre, Paris (Alinari)

b. *Nike of Samothrace* (Winged Victory). Hellenistic

PLATE 16

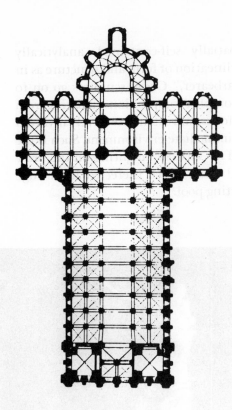

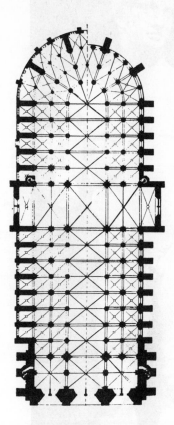

a. Church of St. Sernin, Toulouse.
   Romanesque

b. Cathedral of Notre Dame,
   Paris. Gothic

St. Sernin and Notre Dame are built on the basilica plan with a long nave emphasizing continued northern interest in spatial recession. The earlier Romanesque building shows the analytical tendency toward clear separation of parts (transepts, ambulatory, apsidal chapels, etc.) as contrasted with Gothic fusion of the design into a dominant cellular whole. Bramante started St. Peter's on a central plan, as a Greek cross with equal arms expressing the analytical qualities of balance and equal distribution of emphasis, but it was modified later including the addition of several bays on the western arm, creating a spatially more dynamic composition consistent with Baroque style.

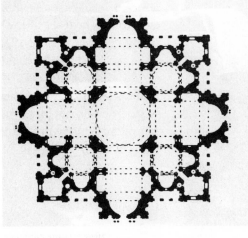

c. Bramante's Design for St. Peter's
   (modified by later architects).
   Renaissance

PLATE 17

a. Andrea Palladio (1518–1580). Church of San Giorgio Maggiore, Venice

b. Cathedral of Notre Dame, Reims

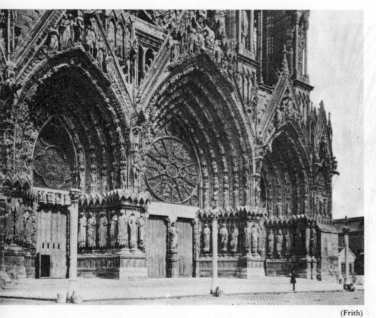

Palladio's design combines two classical temple façades in an attempt to clarify structurally the nave and side aisles of the traditional basilica, and at the same time, to make a fashionable reference to antiquity. Notre Dame's Gothic façade shows the northern affinity for structural complexity, movement, and spatial recession.

PLATE 18

a. Church of St. Peter, Vatican, Rome. Interior of the Nave

(Alinari)

b. Fan vaulting. St. Peter's Cathedral, Exeter

(British Information Service)

The sensational style of later periods and northern art generally is not associated with structural clarity. Hence the clear rib structure of the thirteenth century's four part Gothic vaulting is elaborated in England into "fan vaulting" and for other more complex patterns. The equally vast spaces of the Italian Baroque St. Peter's are contained by more solid forms. A sense of the scale in the latter example may be gained by noting that a person is about as tall as the base of a column.

PLATE 19

a. Animal page from the *Book of Durrow*

b. Cross page from the *Lindisfarne Gospels*

The intricate pattern of these elaborate eighth century manuscripts, illuminated by Irish and Saxon monks, suggests the intensity of their devotional concentration as they turned away from the pain and terror of the real world toward the mystery of salvation in the hereafter.

PLATE 20

a. Jan van Eyck (c. 1385–1440). *Adoration of the Mystic Lamb*. Central Panel of Retable. Church of St. Bavon, Ghent

b. Andrea Verrocchio (1425–1488). *Baptism of Christ*

Both northern and southern Europe still show a high Gothic concern with the mystery of Christian salvation in these fifteenth century paintings. The greater tendency toward analytical expression in the South, however, impels the Italian artists toward a "scientific naturalism" involving detailed study of anatomy and perspective that reflects the contemporary intellectual interests of the Renaissance eventually opposed by the Church.

PLATE 21

c. *Zeus* or *Poseidon*

a. Archaic Greek *Kouros*

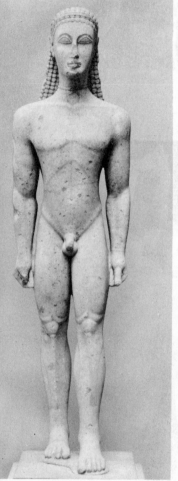

Acropolis Museum, Athens (Alinari)

b. Archaic Greek *Kore*

National Museum, Athens (Alinari)

Courtesy of The Metropolitan Museum of Art,
Fletcher Fund, 1932

Comparison of a number of early Greek works reveals a constant effort to achieve a more convincing visual reality, accounting in some degree for the analytical quality of the style. They also indicate the general affection of Mediterranean cultures for analytical expression, as well as a vestige of the later primitive (neolithic) practice of humanizing environment by geometrical abstractions, even of the human body.

PLATE 22

a. Alessandro Botticelli (1444–1510). *Spring*

c. Same, detail of upraised hands

The beholder's delight in this painting is
not that of his eye, which in this case simply
transmits sensations to the hand. Characteristically the hand moves from part to
part, and that is the way to "feel" the fine
linear contours in this picture. Thus the
general view is less pleasing than in later,
optically fused work.

b. Same, detail of the Three Graces

PLATE 23

a. Titian Vecellio (1477–1576). *Sacred and Profane Love*    Borghese Gallery, Rome (Alinari)

b. Titian Vecellio. *Entombment of Christ*

Museo del Prado, Madrid (Anderson)

The so-called "Sacred and Profane Love" painted by Titian at the height of his career, though less linear than work of his fifteenth-century predecessors, is composed planimetrically, of clear tactile forms. During the course of his own career he evolved the highly optic style seen in the much later "Entombment," with its tonal softening of contours, complex recessional movement of the limbs at an angle to the picture plane, and fusion of the figures into a domelike mass emphasizing the spotlighted body of Christ.

PLATE 24

a.  George Caleb Bingham (1811–1879). *Verdict of the People*

Broad social concern and community
pride in the democratic process are
expressed by the midwestern Bingham in a thoroughly analytical style
of clear linear description, distinction
of parts and planimetric construction
of space. In contrast, the expatriate
Whistler portrays in sensational style
his own personal life, with implications of leisure, luxury, and art for
art's sake in hints of currently fashionable admiration of Japanese art.

PLATE 25

b.  J. A. M. Whistler (1834–1903). *The Artist in the
Studio*

A masterful combination of opposite spatial qualities is shown in this noted Golden-Age composition. The architectural background is constructed in firmly planimetric fashion, but the figures are distributed within it recessionally, moving from the grouped secondary characters in the foreground deep into the implied volume of space, past the two dominant figures of Plato and Aristotle, who alone are silhouetted against the distant sky within the last archway.

Raphael Sanzio (1483–1520). *School of Athens*. The Vatican, Rome

PLATE 26

a.  Nicolas Poussin (1594–1665). *Funeral of Phocion*

Serial attention to detail, pre-dominantly planimetric construction of space, and concern with broad general aspects of natural or social environment indicate the resurgence of a new analytical expression. However, there is more optic concern with tone and other sensuous values than in previous analytical styles. Hogarth's various series of paintings were presented originally to the Foundling Hospital in London, being unsalable to the upper classes which they criticised, and he lived on the sale of engravings to the moralistic lesser bourgeoisie.

b.  William Hogarth (1697–1764). Engraving. *The Countess' Dressing Room,* from the series *Marriage a la Mode*

PLATE 27

These two highly successful paintings in resounding and appropriately analytical style express an early stage of American cultural independence. They may be disparaged as "provincial" only insofar as they fail to achieve the optic virtuosity of fashionable European examples, then widely admired, especially by those Americans who considered themselves expatriate Englishmen.

b. Ammi Phillips (fl. early 19th century).
   *Portrait of Mrs. Almira Perry*

a. John Singleton Copley (1737–1815). *Portrait of the Artist's Family*
   Private Collection

PLATE 28

a. Sir John Millais (1829–1896). *Ophelia*

Analytical style may appear arbitrarily during a period in which dominant cultural interests are more sophisticated and sensuous, as in the work of the "Sunday painter," Rousseau. He was inspired by nineteenth-century individualism to practice in a field for which he did not have full professional preparation. The Pre-Raphaelite Brotherhood in England, as in this work by Millais, attempted academically to recreate the primitive" linear clarity they admired in fifteenth-century Italian painting as "honest craftsmanship," in protest against the artificial pretensions of the current European culture.

b. Henri Rousseau (1844–1910). *The Dream*

PLATE 29

Museum, Cairo

a. *Portrait of the Overseer Ka'aper*
(so-called "Sheik el Beled").
Egyptian Ka statue in wood, Old
Kingdom Museum, Cairo

b. *Baking and Brewing.* Ushabti group from the
tomb of Meket-Re, Thebes

Egyptian funerary art shows a high degree
of skill in literal representation of forms
serving the intense religious concern with
life after death. This was similar to the
early prehistoric artists demonstration of
the community's emotional concentration
on the hunt in naturalistic representations
of the hunted animals.

PLATE 30

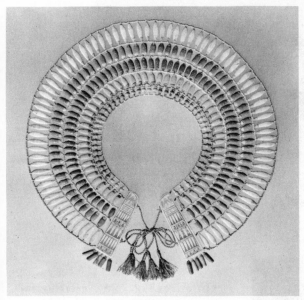

a. Broad collar of faience beads from Thebes

In the decorative arts, the Egyptians demonstrated a desire to humanize their environment by conferring on it a highly geometrical and rhythmic character, somewhat as the neolithic cultures used abstract patterns derived from the crafts to assert their nascent sense of distinctness from and victory over natural environment.

PLATE 31

b. Column with palm leaf capital from Sakkareh

Courtesy of The Metropolitan Museum of Art, Rogers Fund, 1907

a. Processional relief from a tomb at Sakkareh

(Alinari)

Interiors of the ceremonial chambers of Egyptian tombs were covered virtually from floor to ceiling with figures having some practical religious function, usually that of providing the deceased with means of sustenance and activity in the life after death. Early Byzantine mosaics, running the full length of the church, show a somewhat greater sense of decorative distribution, although the coverage of the wall space is also quite complete.

b. *Adoration of the Magi.* Detail from the mosaic decoration of the triforium and clerestory. Church of San Vitale, Ravenna

PLATE 32

a. Baths of Diocletian, Rome. Artist's conception by Paullin

The chief change wrought by the Romans in the culture they inherited from Greece was the elaboration of architecture and sculpture with a pervasive sense of spatial extension, as in the recessional vistas inviting movement from room to room of the monumental baths. The illusion of deep space is implied by the various depths of relief in the figures of Titus' triumphal procession and in the attempt at recessional composition of the archway at the right. (Compare Plates 4 and 9a)

b. *Spoils of Jerusalem*. Relief. Arch of Titus, Rome

PLATE 33

(Alinari)

a. *Christ and the Apostles in Jerusalem.* Apse mosaic. Church of Sta. Pudenziana, Rome

Any question as to whether the severe, unrealistic treatment of the late Byzantine mosaic at Monreale was required by the medium of small glass cubes set in cement, may be answered by noting the highly illusionistic effects of mass and space the Romans had previously achieved in the mosaic medium, as in the fourth-century apse from one of the earliest Christian churches.

(Alinari)

b. *Christos Pantokrator* (Creator of All). Apse mosaic. Cathedral, Monreale

PLATE 34

(Marbourg)

a. *Milling.*

(Caisse Nationale)

b. *Hunting.* Column capitals Church of La Madeleine, Vézelay (1132–1140)

The principal, officially prescribed decoration of the Romanesque church was symbolic of other-worldly concerns; but lesser items like the numerous column capitals, whose design was left to the stone cutters, show a lively realism reflecting a growing concern with the material present.

c. *Descent of the Holy Spirit.* Tympanum. Church of La Madeleine, Vézelay

PLATE 35

The Romanesque portal from the south of France shows the Mediterranean tendency to adhere to an analytical presentation of mass in contrast to the attenuation and fluidity of figures in the northern tympanum of the previous plate. The flowing drapery of the figure of Moses illustrates the northern interest in active linear movement, maintained even as Gothic style becomes more and more realistic.

a.  *Sts. Peter, John the Evangelist, and Trophime.* Main portal. Church of St. Trophime, Arles

(Giraudon)

b. Claes Sluter (d. 1406). *Moses.* Detail from the Well of the Prophets

Museum, Dijon (Giraudon)

PLATE 36

In addition to the elaborate Rococo art of the national court in France during the seventeenth and eighteenth centuries, of which the fused circular composition, central focus, and recessional movement in Boucher's artificial scene are characteristic, there was a steady production of realistic genre painting. The work of Georges de Latour shows a highly analytical concern with firmly formed masses and clear linear outlines despite his frequent use of brilliant effects of illumination.

a. Georges Dumesnil de Latour (1593–1652). *St. Joseph, Carpenter*

Musée du Louvre, Paris (Caisse Nationale)

b. Francois Boucher (1703–1770). *Venus Receiving the Arms of Aenaeas from Vulcan*

Musée du Louvre, Paris (Caisse Nationale)

PLATE 37

a. Jacques Louis David (1748–1825). *Death of Socrates*

The movement toward a better way of life, that grew during the eighteenth century into the French Revolution, inspired a new analytical culture which David's early linear style expresses. As the bourgeoisie solidified their power in the following century, however, the Romantic movement increasingly exploited the aesthetic values of tone and color, and developed new types of subject matter under slogans of realistic freedom from the rules of academic classicism. Frequently, however, they were more like escapist flights from the realities of contemporary existence into remote periods of history, colorful areas of colonial adventure, or the imaginary events of literature.

b. Eugène Delacroix (1798–1863). *Abduction of Rebecca* (Scott's *Ivanhoe*)

PLATE 38

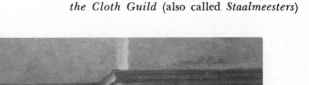
Rijksmuseum, Amsterdam

The practice of group portraiture, exemplified by Rembrandt's painting of a committee of leading textile manufacturers, demonstrates the civic pride of newly republican Holland, and is found throughout bourgeois society in the seventeenth and eighteenth centuries. The Gothic realism from which both pictures stem has become quite optic (cf. Plate 5b). The Vermeer depicts personal aims of luxurious and leisurely domesticity rather than broader or more practical perspectives.

a. Jan Vermeer (1632–1675). *Young Woman Reading a Letter*

b. Rembrandt van Rijn (1606–1669. *Syndics of the Cloth Guild* (also called *Staalmeesters*)

Rijksmuseum, Amsterdam

PLATE 39

a. Honoré Daumier (1808–1879). *Waiting at the Station*

A vastly important aspect of the industrial revolution was the application of steam's mechanical power to transportation. Daumier is here concerned with human emotions aroused by the experience of travel, whereas Monet sees the railroad aesthetically as a novel and entrancing spectacle of lights, colors and textures. (See also Plate 5)

b. Claude Monet (1840–1926).
*Old St. Lazare Station*

PLATE 40

Peter Paul Rubens (1577–1640). *Arrival of Marie de Medicis at Marseilles*. From the series on the *Life of Marie de Medicis*

As the leading painter of aristocratic Flanders, Rubens learned the elegant artificialities of the Renaissance in several years of study and practice in Italy, and added to it a dynamic northern vitality, thus producing a monumental expression of the Baroque style. This series on the life of Henry of Navarre's queen was made in the course of a diplomatic mission by the artist to the court of France.

PLATE 41

a. Pablo Picasso (b. 1881). *Les Demoiselles d'Avignon*

Artists became more and more concerned during the nineteenth century with bringing out aesthetic aspects of the
subjects they painted, until it dawned on them that these
subjective interests might be given priority over literal appearances. Distortions were made either for aesthetic excitement, as in this painting of Picasso's cubist period, or to
enhance emotional connotations. The drama of style in art
could hardly be more striking than in a comparison of Picasso's nudes with Rubens' nymphs in the foreground of the
previous plate and Botticelli's Three Graces (Plate 23b)

PLATE 42

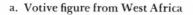

a. Votive figure from West Africa

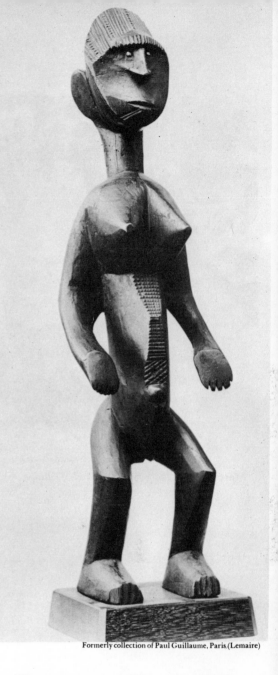

Formerly collection of Paul Guillaume, Paris (Lemaire)

Museum of Modern Art, New York

b. Jacques Lipchitz (b. 1891). Figure

The manner in which this African Negro carving reduces the human figure to elemental geometrical forms was followed by Picasso in his cubist painting shown in the previous plate. However, the Lipchitz figure seems to echo the more completely abstracted burial fetishes.

PLATE 43

Museum of Modern Art, New York

a. Marc Chagall (b. 1887). *I and the Village*

Discovery of the subconscious mind led artists like Chagall to create dreamlike fantasies. Lately artists have claimed similar importance for spontaneous gestures suggesting no identifiable forms whatever, as being motivated by even deeper subconscious impulse.

b. Hans Hoffman (b. 1880). *Delight*

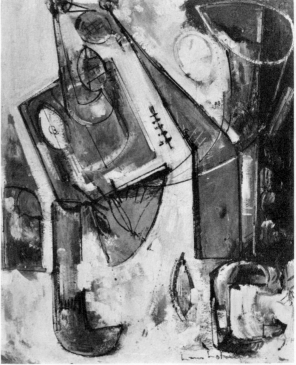

PLATE 44

Museum of Modern Art, New York

Feeling that much was amiss in artificially regimented European society of the early twentieth century, many artists such as those comprising the Dada movement, expressed their protest in sarcastic or shocking combinations as in Ernst's painting. Later this type of expression came to be called "Surrealism" and the feeling of seriousness slipped away.

a. Max Ernst (b. 1891).
   *Napoleon in the Wilderness*

Museum of Modern Art, New York

b. Joan Miro (b. 1893). *Dutch Interior*

Museum of Modern Art, New York

PLATE 45

Courtesy of The Metropolitan Museum of Art, gift of John Wolfe, 1893

a. Alexandre Cabanel (1823–1889).
*Birth of Venus*

b. Willem de Kooning (b. 1904).
*Woman, I*

Eclectic imitation of classical art
continued to be sponsored
throughout the nineteenth century by the École des Beaux Arts
in France and other government
agencies, although the plushy
eroticism of Cabanel's "Venus"
lacks the originality of some un-
official developments and ignores the vigorous advances in
the social and economic life of
its time. Despite its outspoken
antagonism to womanhood, de
Kooning's violent portrayal is
more respectful.

Museum of Modern Art, New York

a. Winslow Homer (1836–1910). *Campfire*

Winslow Homer represents the dignity of Man in various types of struggle with nature, expressing a recently pioneer society still pushing into new lands on it borders. Producers of livestock celebrated their triumphs in seasonal exhibitions as represented by the Currier and Ives print, which is highly analytical not only in the clarified linear description of objects and the planimetric composition, but also in the separate centers of attention such as the trotting race and the stone boat pull in the background.

b. Currier and Ives. *In the County Fair Grounds*

PLATE 47